My Season on the Brink

My Season on the Brink

Brink

A FATHER'S SEVEN WEEKS AS A LITTLE LEAGUE MANAGER

Paul B. Brown

ST. MARTIN'S PRESS   NEW YORK

Design by Judith Christensen

Library of Congress Cataloging-in-Publication Data

Brown, Paul B.
    My season on the brink : a father's seven weeks as a Little League manager / Paul B. Brown.
        p.   cm.
    ISBN 0-312-07639-8
    1. Little League Baseball, inc.   2. Brown, Paul B.   3. Baseball for children—United States—Managers—Biography.   I. Title.
GV880.5.B76A3   1992   92-3596
796.357′62—dc20   CIP

First Edition: May 1992

10 9 8 7 6 5 4 3 2 1

This one's for my parents

Contents

What you are about to read is true. Some of the names, and a couple of details, have been altered in the (probably futile) hope that these changes will allow me to spend the rest of my days living peacefully in town.

My Season on the Brink

1

This Is the Moment I've Dreamed Of?

This was it.

Yes, I knew it was only a game—and only an exhibition game at that. And yes, I knew that nobody other than me would ever care. But this was the moment that managing was all about. Ever since they told me I'd be coaching first and second graders in Little League, I'd been wondering how I'd handle my first major managerial decision. And here—in our very first game—I was about to find out.

To be sure, things had not gone exactly as I had expected. For one thing, nobody had told me that the coaches in this league double as umpires, which leads to some interesting calls. For example, on close plays the tendency is to take turns. "Let's see, your guy was out last time . . . okay, 'He's safe!' " For another, there was a presumption—especially during the practice games—that you would give the worst kids every conceivable benefit of the doubt. "that's strike four, Jeffrey, one more and I am afraid you really will be out."

Still, it was baseball. And while I had promised myself that I would not take all this too seriously, here we were in the bottom of the sixth—the last inning in Little League—and we were ahead by three runs. Visions of Manager of the Year were beginning to flash through my head.

Now if you're the Oakland A's, being ahead by three is just about a sure thing. However, when you play in a league where the final score is often 36-31, three runs don't mean much, as I had already found out in my managerial debut. At differing points during the game we had been ahead 10-3 and 18-14, only to find ourselves trailing an inning or two later.

But we had come back. How? The old-fashioned way: we'd hit the ball to people who couldn't catch. At this age—and all the kids in our league were between six and a half and eight—each team has about three players who have a vague understanding of what baseball is all about. When the ball is hit to somebody else, it becomes an adventure. It's not uncommon for a routine ground ball to second to wind up a triple, and just about everything hit to the outfield is guaranteed to be a home run. Through blind luck—not managerial brilliance, I'm afraid—the balls we hit had tended to find their worst fielders.

Still, the good news was we were ahead by three. Even better, we were only one out away from victory.

The bad news? The bases were loaded, and their best batter, Danny McGrath—all freckles and forearms—was up.

We did, however, have a couple of things in our favor.

2

Danny was the ninth batter of the inning—which meant no matter what, he would be the last person to hit.*

Advantage number two? I had a plan.

I called time and started repositioning the team, putting my son Peter, who, by default, was our best fielder, out in center. In Little League, just like in real baseball, the center fielder is captain of the outfield; anything that's within his reach is rightfully his. And since our left and right fielders tended to daydream, pick dandelions that they made into necklaces, and wave a lot to their parents, our center fielder was essentially responsible for anything hit beyond second base.

During the time-out, I told Peter he should play extremely deep. I wanted to make sure the ball couldn't be hit over his head. That was just the first part of my plan.

"Peter, if the ball is hit to you on the ground," I told him, "just pick it up and throw it home. Don't worry about the kid at third. Even if he scores, we're ahead by two. And if the guy from second scores, we'll still win by a run. The big thing is to keep Danny from scoring. That way we'll get at least a tie, and if you get the ball home before the kid at first gets there, we'll win."

"Dad, I know that. Everybody knows that," Peter said in a tone that made it clear the situation was well in hand. "Come on."

With that, the game resumed. Danny McGrath swung at

---

*The rules say you can only send up nine kids to hit in an inning. No matter how many people are out, or where the ball is hit, the ninth batter must run completely around the bases. If he stops, or is tagged out before making it home, he's out. The nine-batter rule is an attempt to hold the score down and keep the game moving. Without it, given the level of defense, it would be possible for one team to hit all day. As it was, we were already winning 28-25.

3

the first pitch, and I couldn't have diagrammed it any better. He hit a solid three-hopper up the middle, the kind of thing Peter could handle in his sleep. Peter would catch the ball, throw it home, and we'd win. The New York Yankees would somehow hear of my brilliant managerial moves, send the limo to pick me up, and come next spring, I'd be in Fort Lauderdale talking with reporters about how I was going to restore Yankee pride, how we would be stressing the fundamentals and concentrating on "hitting that short porch out in right field," and maybe even . . .

What was this?

I wasn't sure at first. All I saw was a blur coming from left field—the same left field where Justin Marconi had spent the entire game looking longingly at the ice cream truck parked just beyond the foul line. Every thirty seconds or so Justin would ask "Is the game over yet? I want to get a Fat Frog," which I took to mean some kind of ice cream bar, and not another addition to Justin's critter collection.

When he wasn't asking for ice cream, Justin spent his time out in left field on his hands and knees digging for ants, beetles, grubs, and anything else he could find crawling underground. It wasn't uncommon for him to run off the field—in the middle of an inning—to show his mother what he had dug up. It got so that I didn't even bother calling time when he jogged off to display his latest discovery. We'd play without a left fielder until Justin's mother could convince him to head back onto the field. You can get used to just about anything as a Little League manager.

But here was Justin—funny little Justin, whose only interest up until now was separating the heads of worms from their bodies—sweet kind Justin, who had never, *ever* showed any interest in having anything to do with a ball hit within five feet of him, let alone one he would have to run for—sprinting, *sprinting* toward the ball.

"Ohmigod, Justin, go back!"

Justin, to be charitable, was not our best fielder—to be honest nobody had ever seen him catch anything other than worms—yet he had suddenly chosen this moment—this pivotal moment in my first game as a manager—to become a hero. You could see it in his eyes. He was going to get to that ball, throw it home, and have his teammates carry him off the field on their shoulders. He'd be a star. They'd mention his name in the same breath as Rickey Henderson and Jose Canseco. It would be even better than killing worms and eating Fat Frogs. He was going to catch that ball. Little Justin Marconi may have headed out to left field as a skinny six-year-old with straight brown hair that always fell over his eyes, but he was going to come back *a star*!

Now clearly this was going to be trouble. There was no telling what might happen if Justin actually got to the ball. Earlier in the game, he had picked up a grounder—well, actually he waited for it to stop rolling—and then promptly threw it behind him. An inning later he got to another ball and just held it, as the other team circled the bases in what seemed like slow motion.

It was frightening to think what might happen now that the game was on the line.

"Justin, stop!"

For a moment I thought we'd be okay. The ball was hit far closer to Peter than Justin, so there was no chance that Justin would get to it first. But apparently Justin understood that too, because just as Peter fielded the ball, Justin hurled his body through the air and let loose a scream last heard in a

5

John Wayne movie just before the kamikaze pilot rammed the aircraft carrier.

If he couldn't get the ball, Justin reasoned, then nobody would. He would tackle Peter, wrestle the ball away from him, and save the day.

"Justin, no!"

Now Peter was seven, compared to Justin's six, and had about six inches and fifteen pounds on his teammate. But you can never underestimate the speed and strength of a six-year-old who's possessed. Screaming all the way, Justin flew through the air—arms outstretched—and executed a tackle that would have made Vince Lombardi proud. Once he had Peter down, Justin held onto Peter's arms for dear life and actually managed to knock the ball free at one point.

By the time Peter threw Justin off and retrieved the ball, all four runs had scored.

We had lost. Final score: 29-28.

Justin never really explained why he did what he did. He complained a little about how the ball rarely was hit out to left field, and how he was tired of digging for worms; then he asked if he could go home.

As for Peter and the team, the loss was no big deal. After all, they'd see Danny McGrath and the rest of their friends on the other team at school in the morning.

The parents took it pretty well, too—although two of them did make a point of reminding me that my career managerial record was now 0-1.

And me? I felt a little better after I finished my Fat Frog. (I bought one for everyone on the team. They're not bad: pistachio ice cream, shaped like a frog. They use M&Ms for the eyes, nose, and mouth.)

Still, as I drove Peter back to our house, I started to wonder for the first time exactly *what* I had gotten myself into.

2

How Did I End Up with a Whistle Around My Neck?

In the words of an old Whittier College football manager, let me make this perfectly clear: I was the most average athlete imaginable as a kid.

If there was a race, you could count on me finishing in the middle of the pack. A push-up contest involving ten guys? I'd be the one who did fifth best. The ever-popular rope-climb in gym? I'd get to the top, but it would take awhile. (And I never did figure out how to get back down without suffering rope burn.)

I loved sports and played them all the time when I was growing up in the suburbs surrounding Manhattan, and to this day I can still recite—in less than three seconds—the NY Yankees 1961 starting lineup. Richardson, Kubek, Maris, Mantle, Berra, Howard, Skowron, Boyer, and the pitcher, who always seemed to be Whitey Ford. In my defense, 1961

7

was the year I discovered baseball (I was seven) and the Yankee lineup never changed.

But despite my fascination with sports, I was about as far from being a natural athlete as you could get. By throwing a football through a tire for hours on end, dribbling a soccer ball up and down my backyard a hundred times every day, or throwing a baseball against a wall at school until it was too dark to see, I was able to turn myself into someone who was perfectly adequate. I wasn't awful. Merely fair.

I did, however, play two sports reasonably well, but even there I never gave future Bo Jacksons any sleepless nights. In basketball, I was on a "Y" team that finished 14-16 in its best year, and I played an okay game of tennis. And while it's true that if you let me have more than two drinks, I will bore everyone within earshot about how I was offered a tennis scholarship to college, the truth is that's a lot less impressive than it sounds.

The offer came from a major football powerhouse that was constantly under investigation by the NCAA for awarding scholarships to kids who couldn't read or write. In a fit of inspiration, the athletic director figured out a way to solve the problem. Instead of recruiting smarter—if less athletically gifted—football players, he'd hide how dumb they really were.

Traditionally, colleges release the high-school grades and test scores of their student-athletes team by team. Since the football players at this school typically had straight D's and combined SAT scores in the low 700s (out of a possible 1600), it was pretty obvious that a lot of the kids who were starting on the defensive line had no business being in any college, let alone this one, which, with the exception of its football players, held incoming students to pretty high academic standards.

But while the rules said you had to tell the world how well your student-athletes did in high school, they didn't require that test scores be broken out according to team.

Here was an opportunity, the athletic director thought. He'd pool the results of every student-athlete he had. The grades and test scores of the kids on the lacrosse, baseball, and women's field hockey teams would help offset the numbers turned in by his football players. This way he could continue to give scholarships to the nation's best high-school football players—regardless of race, creed, or academic ability.

The key to making this work was recruiting reasonably smart swimmers, wrestlers, and tennis players. And that's how I got the scholarship offer. Believe me, my grades were far better than my backhand.

I turned down the scholarship, by the way. But that decision wasn't made out of any sense of moral purity. I would have been thrilled to go to school on an athletic scholarship, thinking, like all red-blooded seventeen-year-olds everywhere, I reasoned it would be easier to pick up girls, once I let be it known, oh-so-casually, that I was a varsity jock. No, I turned down the scholarship to keep from turning blue.

While the alumni made sure that the football team had the best training facilities in the world—there were three regulation-sized, indoor, heated practice fields, for example—minor sports, such as tennis, didn't fare so well. Not only did the tennis coach actually have to teach (chemistry, as it turned out), but there were no training facilities or indoor courts. Since snow covered the campus from November through April, that meant practice usually began with you holding a shovel, not a racquet.

While I dreamed of fame and glory on the pro tennis circuit—to give you an idea of how long ago this was, Rod

Laver, Arthur Ashe, and the doubles team of Stan Smith and Bob Lutz were my heroes—I wasn't willing to risk frostbite to achieve it. My parents, bless them, ended up paying four years' tuition at a good school that would never dream of sullying its reputation by taking sports seriously.

I tell you all this because I want you to know that I didn't become a coach to: a. Recapture some faded glory. I never heard a crowd chant my name. I averaged exactly three points a game in basketball and if we had a dozen people watch us during our tennis matches, it was a lot. Or b. To get even for always being the last one picked in gym. I was never picked last. I was always tenth in a field of twenty.

The truth is I signed up to be an *assistant* coach to help save my son from being subjected to guys who fell into either category a. or b. I figured if anyone was going to yell at my kid, it was going to be me, and I had absolutely no intention of yelling at Peter or anybody else. Little League is supposed to be a time when kids learn a bit about the fundamentals of baseball and have some fun. I signed up to help make sure that would happen for Peter and his friends. I was no longer a sports fanatic—I still follow the Yankees when I can, but for the life of me, I couldn't begin to guess at their current starting lineup, let alone recite it quickly—and I wasn't going to have some frustrated jock take out all his Walter Mitty fantasies on my kid.

I ended up being a head coach by default. They couldn't find enough parents who could spend the minimum six to eight hours a week coaching required. We have two games, plus a practice, and it's hard for most people to find that kind of time, especially when it requires getting home by late afternoon during the week, since that's when most of our practices and games are held.

My son overheard a couple of the other parents talking

about the problem they were having getting enough managers and said, "My dad can do it. He never goes to work."

Since then I've explained to Peter that just because I write at home a couple of days a week does not mean I'm unemployed. Still, the township was desperate and the next thing I know I'm on the phone with the league president who's telling me that "draft night" is two weeks away, and she's looking forward to meeting me. Before I can explain that all I really want to do is *assist*—you know, help out, maybe keep score, work with the infielders, that sort of thing?—she's telling me that she'll have team uniforms and bats and balls waiting, and she's off the phone.

Gulp.

I've never coached anything in my life.

Peter, what have you done?

3

Draft Night: Or the Longest Day Had Nothing on Us

It should have taken a half hour.

Prior to the start of each season, every kid going out for Little League is rated, on a scale of one to ten, on their ability to hit, field, and throw. First graders, who have never played before, show up on a Saturday for a quick audition. The coaches rate second graders based on how well they played the year before.

Each kid's name and score are put on an index card, and the cards are ranked in numerical order—all the "30"s are put on top, then the "29"s, and so forth. On draft night, the coaches gather to find out who's going to be on their team. We sit around someone's kitchen table and the cards are dealt out in order, starting with the "30"s. That way the kids are distributed evenly on the basis of their ability. After everyone has his team, we then check for potential conflicts. Are there brothers who have to be together? Did the kids whose parents are going to car-pool end up on the same team? That sort of thing.

The real purpose of draft night is social. You meet your fellow coaches, figure out who's going to have practice when, tell a couple of stories about what the Justin Marconis of the world did last season, and then you go home and dream of having an undefeated season.

That's what they told me was going to happen anyway. Remember, this was my first draft night, and the idea of meeting everyone sounded fine to me—as long as it didn't take too long. I had a six-hour plane ride the next day, and I was hoping to get to bed early.

Fat chance.

The meeting was at the home of Sherry Cavise, the league president, and when I showed up at 7:00 P.M. I fully expected to be out of there by eight. I got home at 1:30 A.M.

You never could have guessed that was going to happen by the way the evening started. It began simply enough. Each of the eleven guys who was going to coach introduced himself. I knew some of them from the swim club, or because their kid was—or had been—in Peter's class.

Just so you know exactly how ridiculous the evening would become, let me tell you a little bit about my hometown and the people who were sitting in Sherry Cavise's kitchen.

I live in Holmdel, New Jersey, which is on the northernmost part of the New Jersey shore, about fifty miles south of Manhattan. The township is eighteen square miles and has all of nine thousand people. I haven't checked recently, but my guess is the number of horses, cows, and sheep in town probably equals the number of residents, and pine trees and evergreens outnumber us about two thousand to one. We're the place everyone comes when it's time to buy their Christmas tree; we are the living definition of the boonies.

Now for a lot of my friends, especially the ones who grew up and still live in Manhattan, Holmdel is hopelessly quaint—the kind of place they might visit on a Sunday afternoon drive—but live there? Please.

But for other people—especially overachievers in their late thirties and early forties who have kids—Holmdel is Mecca. The schools are wonderful—Bell Labs is our biggest employer and the hundreds of astrophysicists, electrical engineers, and various and sundry Ph.D.'s it employs make sure that the school district remains among the top rated in the state.

Until recently, the township required that each house be on at least two acres of land. There's no crime—DWI arrests and fender benders still make page one of the local weekly newspaper—no pollution, and only an occasional traffic light.

Given all this, it was just a matter of time before the township was discovered by high-powered New York executives looking for a better place to live.

The men gathered around Sherry Cavise's kitchen table—this season they were all men, although we've had a few mothers who've coached—were representative of the folks you'd find in Holmdel. As I said, there were eleven of us, average age about thirty-seven. Professions? One dentist, two Wall Street lawyers (one security, the other tax), three people who owned their own business (optical supply, construction, and a distribution company), a mid-level insurance executive, a Bell Labs Ph.D., a printing company sales manager, a former real estate developer now involved in various entrepreneurial projects, and me, someone who's spent most of his professional life writing for business magazines such as *Forbes, Business Week,* and *Inc.* Later on more fathers would

14

join this group, as assistant coaches. What we all had in common was that each of our sons (since there was also a separate girls softball league, girls only made up a small percentage of our league) would be one of the 125 kids playing baseball during the next seven weeks.

This could be fun, I thought as I introduced myself. I'll meet some new people, and maybe find somebody to play tennis with. But the most important thing was that we all believed in the same thing: our job was to teach the kids the basics and make sure they had a good time. There'd be no pressure about winning and losing; no yelling about balls thrown to the wrong base; no temper tantrums if a kid makes an error or the umpire blows a call. Just fun, with a little instruction thrown in. That's why I had signed up, and for the life of me, I couldn't figure out why anyone would take the "first and second grade instructional baseball league," as we were officially billed, more seriously than that.

Boy, was I naive. I found out exactly how much of an innocent I was when Sherry began dealing out the index cards.

"Wait a minute," said Chris, the construction company owner, who was sitting across the table from me. "Why don't we make sure that the numbers are in order?"

Since there were 125 kids, that would take about ten or fifteen minutes, but hey, if that's what they wanted to do— to make doubly sure that the kids were evenly distributed— it was fine with me. I looked at my watch and thought, Okay, home by eight-thirty, no problem.

But there were lots of problems.

For one thing, who would get the first card? While the first couple of kids were rated as "30"s, the scores fell off rapidly after that.

"Whoever picks last, which means he gets the eleventh card, is going to be starting at a *huge* disadvantage,"

15

said Bill, the insurance exec. "What are we going to do about it?"

Some background is in order. The ratings are almost totally subjective. You and I might watch the same kid throw the ball and I might rate his throwing ability at "7," and you could give him an "8" or even a "9." And the same holds true for fielding and hitting.

What this realistically means is there isn't a whole lot of difference between someone who's rated a "17" and someone who has a "20" printed on the back of his card. Since that's true, and since the #11 kid in the pack had a rating of "22"—compared to the "30" given to #1—it was hard to see where there'd be the "huge disadvantage" that Bill was talking about.

However he—and to be fair, two or three others—were determined not to get "stuck" with the eleventh kid in the deck.

We ended up putting eleven numbers in a hat and decided to receive our cards based on the number we drew. I got #11. Before all this silliness started, I wouldn't have minded. But by the time I got my highest-rated kid, a "22," I began to have my doubts. Maybe those eight points really did represent a huge difference. One superstar has been known to carry a team. Maybe I had been set up.

That's ridiculous, I told myself. There's no reason to be paranoid. We're all here to have fun. By the time the rest of the cards had been dealt, I had calmed down.

I didn't stay that way for long.

Right or wrong, every father coaches his own son. And our eleven kids, like all the rest, were ranked on a scale of one to thirty and placed in the stack of index cards. That meant that each father/coach had a one-in-eleven chance of getting his son.

What that also meant was we'd have to do a lot of trading, once the cards were dealt, to make sure that every father ended up with his own kid.

I figured I'd go first.

"Who has Peter Brown?" I asked in all innocence.

"I do," said Bill, the insurance executive, who had been sitting there with his arms folded and a smug look on his face, ever since he had drawn #2 out of the hat.

"Great," I said. "I don't have your kid, do I?"

He looked through my index cards. "No."

"Okay, you give me Peter and—" I never got to finish the thought.

"I can't give you Peter," Bill said.

"Why not?"

"Because he's a 'twenty-four' and you don't have anyone who's a 'twenty-four.' "

As I said, my highest-ranked player was a "22." I promptly offered Tommy Griffin to Bill.

"But he's a 'twenty-two.' "

Bill had me there. Tommy was indeed a "22."

"Bill, he's the best kid I got."

"But he's only a 'twenty-two,' " said Bill.

This went on for another three minutes—honest—and finally I said, "Can we do a two-player deal? You give me Peter and somebody else, and I'll give you my 'twenty-two' and somebody else, and we'll make sure the *total* points come out equal. Can you live with that?"

He could. After searching through my cards and Bill's, I ended up trading my "22" and an "18" for Peter and a "16."

Elapsed time of the deal: sixteen minutes.

Now, while all this was going on, the other coaches were going through similar machinations to get their own sons. Often it involved doing a three- or a four-way trade.

By 9:00 P.M., an hour and a half after we had begun handing out the cards, everyone had his own kid. Great, I thought. Time to go home.

Wrong. We still had to deal with the kids of assistant coaches.

Every manager is assigned one or two assistants, and again, there is only a one-in-eleven chance that you've drawn your assistant's kid. So, more trading. It might have been my imagination, but it seemed that Chris, the construction company owner, chose his two assistants based on how highly their kids were rated. But maybe it was a coincidence that both their kids scored in the low "20"s. Then it took another forty-five minutes to get all the siblings and neighbors together.

By eleven, the rosters were finally set and I was yawning and ready to leave. Just as I started to pick up my sweater and head for the door, Bill—a man I was quickly learning to hate—spoke up again.

"Can we just go over the teams, just to make sure they're fair?"

Now, I had absolutely no idea what he was talking about.

I soon found out. Everybody laid out their index cards, and one at a time the other ten coaches took turns analyzing the rosters.

"Freddie McWilliams is a 'twenty-seven'?" Lou, the sales manager, asked. "No way, that kid's a 'thirty' at the very least."

"What's Johnny Kelly doing as a 'fourteen,' the kid's a solid 'twenty,' " asked Jeffrey, the dentist.

While this was going on, Bob, a friend from the swim club, took a look at my team.

"Justin Marconi, Paul, isn't a 'fifteen,' " Bob whispered.

"He's maybe a 'six.' You're going to have to get his rating changed. Trade him if you can."

And so it went for the next hour and a half. The rating of every kid was examined and a coach either demanded a trade for a better kid, if he thought the rating a kid on his team had received was too high, or fought to defend a rating that undervalued one of his better players.

I stayed out of it for the most part. For one thing, it was now after midnight and I was sleepy; I normally go to bed around ten. For another, Bill's and Chris's protestations aside, I still didn't see how much of a difference all of this trading and rerating was going to make. It looked—based on the ratings and the little I knew about some of my kids—like I had a couple of kids who could play, so I figured we'd end up being okay.

I did trade to get rid of a kid I didn't like, David Falcone, a whiner, and got a friend of Peter's, Stevie Moreno, in return. Since David was a "21" and Stevie a "19," everyone thought I was nuts. But I didn't care. I figured Peter and Stevie would be happy, and besides, I just wanted to go home.

Finally, at one-thirty in the morning, after it seemed that every kid had been traded at least three times, the wheeling and dealing was done and we all started to leave.

As we were walking to our cars, Bill, with absolutely no trace of irony, called out to everyone: "Remember, we're just here to make sure everybody has fun."

4

The First Practice: The Phrase "A Comedy of Errors" Suddenly Has New Meaning

"I always start practice by numbering the bases."

That statement, from a neighbor who had been coaching for ten years, had been rattling around my head ever since I got the phone call telling me that I was going to be in charge of a team.

"What are you talking about?" I had asked him.

"It's simple," said Tom, the father of three, who coached everything from soccer to track as his kids grew up. "The first year I was coaching Little League, I laid out the bases. Then I had the kids line up and said, 'To warm up, let's have everybody jog around the base paths.' The first four kids took off toward third. Ever since, I've numbered the bases and explained that you have to run them in order. You'd be amazed at the number of kids who go directly from first to third by cutting across the pitching mound."

I figured Tom was exaggerating; his story about the bases had to be a coach's version of a fish story, or the kind of thing you tell new managers just to scare them.

True, I didn't expect everyone on my team to be as sports obsessed as Peter. That wouldn't be possible.

I once came downstairs at six on a Saturday morning to find Peter, who had just turned five, sprawled on the family-room couch watching television. That wasn't unusual. Peter has never needed much sleep. And I didn't find the fact that the set was tuned to a soccer game to be anything out of the ordinary either. Peter, as everyone in our family has always known, will watch anything with a ball in it. I dare you to find another small child on the planet who will *willingly* sit through an entire golf match. Besides, I told myself as Peter stared intently at the screen, the kid has just started playing soccer, so of course he'd watch a match on TV.

But while watching a soccer game on the TV at 6:00 A.M. made perfect sense to me, what I couldn't understand was why he had the sound turned off. When I turned up the volume, I understood. The game was being broadcast in Spanish. Actually, it was being broadcast in Portuguese (France was playing Brazil in Brazil) and being dubbed into Spanish, for the New York station Peter had on.

I thought, All right, we've reached an all-time low here. However, just as I started to change the channel in search of Saturday morning cartoons, Peter stopped me. "Dad, don't turn it off now. Green's ahead two to one. I want to see if they win." Convinced he was making it up, I poured myself a cup of coffee and sat down next to Peter and watched the game. Sure enough, green (Brazil) was ahead 2-1—periodically they'd flash the score on the screen, which, given my knowledge of Portuguese, or Spanish, for that matter, was a good thing—and Brazil, indeed, held on to win.

Okay, I thought, after Tom told me his story. Not everyone—thank God—is going to be like Peter. And sure, not everyone is going to know the intricacies of the infield fly rule. But the kids have to know at least some of the basics and I'll be able to teach them the rest, right?

Wrong.

The first practice wasn't a total disaster—but it was close, even though I had numbered the bases just to be safe. We had eleven kids out on the field and if one could catch, he couldn't throw. If he could throw, you could be sure he had no idea how to play the game. Hitting the person with the ball to get them out—"pegging" as it was called by the kids— proved to be very popular during the first couple of practices, despite all my explanations to the contrary.

And then we had a couple of kids who couldn't do much of anything. A quick rundown of our roster will give you an idea:

Takeshi Fujiwara. A total unknown. His father worked for the Japanese telephone company and was part of an exchange program with Bell Labs. His family had arrived in March, and Takeshi, who couldn't speak a word of English, was put into Peter's class. Everyone knew Takeshi was bright. My wife, who was one of five people in town who worked with him in school one morning a week, reported that he already could handle fractions, something that had most other second graders baffled, but that's all we knew about him. He didn't speak English, although he seemed to understand it pretty well.

His fielding was fine and his throws were accurate—up to about fifteen feet. After that they fell straight to the ground. His hitting, though, could cause a problem. Takeshi was the smallest kid on the team and even the lightest Little League bat I could find looked awfully big for him when he stood up at the plate. Worse, apparently he had once been held captive and forced to memorize the swings of America's greatest homerun hitters. Every time he got up to bat, he swung as hard as he could—and missed.

Tommy Foley. A perfectly nice eight-year-old (the players ranged in age from six and a half to eight) whom I ended up with totally by accident. I thought he was somebody else.

I had been an assistant soccer coach the previous fall, and one of the kids I liked a lot was—I thought—named Tommy Foley. (After the first practice, where you check all the names against a roster, you never use anyone's last name again.)

Tommy was funny, tried hard, and listened to our meager attempts at strategy. On draft night, he was the kid I thought I was acquiring in a trade. He wasn't. The kid I was thinking of was Tommy *Farley*. Tommy *Foley* turned out to be a perfectly fine little kid who at our first practice couldn't hit a baseball except by accident.

Bobby Foley. Tommy's cousin turned out to be the best athlete on the team, even though I got him, too, by fluke. On the sign-up sheet, Tommy's mother had requested that he and Bobby be on the same team, so they could car-pool together. Once I traded for Tommy, Bobby came along for the ride, as it were. Since Bobby was rated a "15," none of the other coaches cared.

Naturally coordinated, Bobby, who was only seven, was unnaturally strong. He used a 29-ounce bat, compared to 21- to 26-ounce ones used by the rest of our team. The difference may not sound like much, but there are pros—including a couple of homerun hitters such as Jack Clark and Eric Davis—who use bats that *only* weigh 29 ounces.

The other great thing about Bobby was that he called me

23

"Coach" all the time. "Coach, can we scrimmage now?" "Coach, can I play shortstop next inning?" "Coach, how about we try . . ."

Yes, I had sworn at the outset that I was only in this for fun, but I had to admit that being called coach was kind of cool.

Michael Roman. Here was a player. At least during our practices. Michael was one of those kids who had got big early, plus he always had the advantage of being one of the oldest kids in the class.

Holmdel, like a lot of other school districts, has an October thirty-first cut-off for enrollment. Anyone born between November first and December thirty-first has to wait until the next school year to begin kindergarten.

Michael was born November fifth, meaning that he was close to two full years older than some of the kids in the league, and it showed. He was almost a full foot taller than Takeshi, for example.

Even better, I thought at first, than his size was the fact that his father was a sports fanatic. Although I had long since outgrown that phase, Frank Roman hadn't. While the bad news was that Frank's obsession meant that occasionally I was subjected to an analysis of an upcoming, "pivotal" Chicago Cubs–San Diego Padres series, the good news was he had taught Michael the basics—and more. The kid was making backhand catches during infield drills and hit a dozen pitches in a row beyond second base—no mean feat at this age.

I mentally penciled in Michael as our first baseman—a key position in Little League, as you'll see—and cleanup hitter. Here was the kid I was sure would be our star.

John McCarthy. Yet another unknown. He was young— he'd turn seven during the season—and, not surprisingly, had a short attention span. It wasn't unusual during practice for him to just wander off to the swing set nearby. (We practiced behind the elementary school.)

John also had a problem remembering when he was supposed to hit. While I always made it a point to announce the batting order (Peter, first, Takeshi, second, Bobby, third, etc.), John always came to me when we were up and asked "Do I hit this inning?" Then, invariably, when it *was* his turn to bat, somebody would have to go over and call him down from the jungle gym.

Justin Marconi. At the time, I didn't know of Justin's worm collection and his penchant for digging up, as opposed to playing, left field. He just looked like a cute kid with long brown bangs who seemed happy to be out in the sunshine. And while he couldn't throw or catch very well, he sure could hit. In fact, he was responsible for the "Justin Marconi Rule of Pitching."

If you've ever tried playing baseball with someone under two, you'll instantly understand how the rule works.

Toddlers want to play baseball in the worst way—and that's usually how they do it. Since there's no way someone twenty months old is ever going to hit a ball thrown to them, what you quickly learn to do is aim the ball at their bat. That way they at least hit an occasional foul ball and are thrilled.

Well, as it turns out, it's no different in Little League. Since the coaches double as pitchers—not only during practice but during the games as well—you really don't have to worry about too many kids striking out. If the kid is truly awful, you just aim your pitch at his bat, or as the Justin Marconi rule suggests, where they are most likely to swing.

Most kids, when they are first learning to hit, swing the bat funny. Some use it as a tomahawk, always chopping down on the ball. Others have swings that resemble a pendulum: the kid starts with the bat down at his ankles, as if he were

25

holding a golf club, and then swings upward in an arclike motion.

Everybody had their own peculiar quirk. For example, Justin, a right-handed hitter, would always move his front (left) foot backward just before he'd swing. After a couple of weeks of trying to correct the problem with no success, I figured it was just easier to pitch to it. I'd throw the ball inside, and Justin would consistently hit the ball hard to the left side of the field.

Seeing how well Justin did, once I adjusted to him instead of forcing him to adjust to me, I created the Justin Marconi rule, which says coaches must take advantage of the hitter's flaw. So kids like John McCarthy, who chopped down on the ball, always got high pitches to hit. Others like Michael Roman, who always swung from the ankles, got low ones.

At some point—when the kids got bigger and more coordinated—coaches would be able to correct the flaws in their swings fairly easily. As it stood now, there was no way that Justin could ever hit an outside pitch. But for the time being, the Justin Marconi rule would help build my players' confidence and keep them from striking out.

Stevie Moreno. Here was the kid I was most worried about. On the surface, you wouldn't think that would be the case. Stevie lived in a house nearby, is a good friend of Peter's, and is the nicest kid you'd ever meet. He was quiet, had wonderful manners, and got along with absolutely everyone.

So what was the problem? In three words: Steven Moreno, Sr.

Steve Moreno, a salesman's salesman, had a great sense of humor and was levelheaded about everything except his son. Where everybody saw Stevie as a nice little kid, an average ballplayer who had just turned seven and was on the small side, his father saw him as a combination of Mickey Mantle and Ozzie Smith. To hear his father tell it, there had never been a better athlete.

Even the couple of times when Peter, big Steve, Stevie, and I played Whiffle ball in our backyard—where Stevie consistently struck out and had problems catching anything—had failed to change Steve's opinion. Stevie, according to Dad, was going to be our starting shortstop and bat third or fourth.

Oh, joy.

Michael Goodman. Here was a sweet kid who tried hard but the plain fact was that he was much too young. He was born on October thirty-first, which made him barely six and a half, and this was his first participation in any organized activity other than school.

His parents weren't particularly interested in sports. Added to that, he was the oldest child, so that he didn't grow up having older brothers or sisters to copy when it came to sports or anything else. My daughter, Shannon, who is five years younger than Peter, had stopped "throwing like a girl" by the time she was three, and insisted on getting a red football helmet, in addition to a complete ballet outfit, for her fourth birthday.

In a new environment, surrounded by kids he didn't know, Michael spent virtually all his time during the first practice three steps from my side. His parents may have thought that playing on a baseball team was a good idea, but Michael wasn't so sure.

Wei Yang. A total enigma. He was tall and skinny, even for an eight-year-old. By the third practice I started thinking of him as "Sybil" because I never knew which one of him would show up. There were times that he resembled the

27

second coming of Joe DiMaggio. He'd effortlessly glide after fly balls and catch them one-handed. On those days when he came to bat, he'd hit line-drives to all fields.

But then there were the days when he'd trip over first base and not go after a fly ball that landed five feet away.

Despite what seemed like hours of talking to him, I never did figure out the cause for his split athletic personality.

That was the roster, except for Agam Chakavarty—who had been unrated during draft night (meaning he registered to play after the tryouts had ended) and wasn't at the first practice—and, of course, Peter.

Introductions over, it was finally time to go to work, and the only word to describe it was funny. Michael Goodman and Justin couldn't catch anything, Takeshi kept swinging from his heels, and Michael Roman's father was always about two feet away from him shouting "encouragement." "No, Mikey, bend your knees when you field"; "Mikey, step into the throw"; "Mikey, next time . . ." And I think that of the hundred routine ground balls I hit, about thirty were fielded and thrown back near enough to me so that I could catch them without doing my Rudolph Nureyev impression. Nobody told me *I* was going to be sore after our first practice.

Still, there were a couple of bright spots. Michael Roman (who was destined for the rest of year to be known as "Michael Roman" to differentiate him from Michael Goodman), Bobby, and Peter could catch—although Peter was not above rushing in from center field to grab a ball hit slowly toward second base. And with the exception of Tommy Foley and Michael Goodman, everybody could hit at least a little.

While the 1927 Yankees wouldn't have to worry about their place in history, it looked like we wouldn't be embarrassed.

I felt pretty good as the first practice ended.

Little did I know.

5

My Assistant: The Coach from Hell

Part of it was my fault. I've never been good at managing a staff. Either I don't give the people who work for me enough responsibility because I reserve the important things for myself (to make sure that they're done right), or I give them much too much to do and then hover over them and get in the way.

I am, in short, not the easiest person to work for.

But with Little League I swore it would be different. For one thing, I had a role model.

Part of my problem as a department head was that I didn't know how a manager in a *Fortune* 500 company was supposed to act. I never knew anyone who worked effectively within a big company. But I knew *exactly* what a baseball manager was supposed to do. I had grown up watching Ralph Houk and Yogi Berra manage the Yankees.

And the more I thought about how pro teams were run, the

happier I became. Why? Because big league managers have found efficient ways to divide up the work. There are pitching coaches, hitting instructors, bullpen coaches to work with the relievers, and so on down the line.

If it worked for them, it would work for me. Depending on how many coaches I ended up with, I'd divide up the tasks along the same clear lines. Somebody would work with the infielders, somebody else would help the outfielders, and, in addition to making out the lineup and such, I'd serve as the batting instructor. Remember, there were no pitchers to worry about, since the coaches pitch.

That was my goal. And then I met THE COACH FROM HELL.

While you occasionally hear of a pro ballplayer who coaches Little League once he retires—Tommy John, who pitched for the Yankees and Dodgers, does, and Hall of Famer Rod Carew made a second career out of coaching his daughters—that is extremely rare. Invariably the coaches aren't former athletes but parents. That was certainly true in Holmdel and, in fact, the league organizers made sure of it.

On the application you filled out to register your child for Little League, you found the following sentence (the italics are in the original):

Understanding that HYAA (Holmdel Youth Athletic Association) is a public, non-profit organization whose activities are managed, conducted and supervised by volunteers who donate freely of their time and talents solely for the benefit of the participants, I volunteer my time and efforts *for at least one* of the following:

And then you were given a choice of checking off everything from league president to "team parent," one of the people

30

who'd volunteer to bring the refreshments; oranges and water were the two of choice.

I'd like to think all the parents would have been happy to help out even if it hadn't been "required," but the township was taking no chances.

Printed right below the list of volunteer activities, in bold-face type, was:

IMPORTANT: Failure to volunteer and carry out one of these tasks may result in your child's exclusion from our program.

Since no one wanted to go home and have to say, "Well, you see, Johnny, the reason you can't play Little League like the rest of your friends is because Mom and I never got around to volunteering to help out," we always got 100 percent compliance, even if most people volunteered to bring oranges.

Now, one of the choices you could check was "coach" or "assistant coach." Not surprisingly, given the time commitment involved—in addition to being at all the games and practices, the head coach must attend draft night, all coaches meetings, and call his players any time the games are canceled due to rain or scheduling conflicts—most parents interested in coaching checked the box marked "assistant."

But what I discovered was there were a handful of men—and they were all men—who apparently looked at this sign-up form differently. To them, coaching Little League could be their chance to start working their way up the ladder that had "professional baseball manager" marked on the top rung.

It's not as goofy as it sounds. Pay particular attention to the next pro football game that's on TV. Invariably, the announcers will get around to talking about the coach's career and mention that he began by heading up the high-school junior varsity at someplace like Hardscrapple, Texas. That's pretty typical. A coach usually begins at the high-school level, then lands a job as a college assistant, and eventually works his way up through the ranks—line coach, quarterback coach, offensive coordinator—to become a head college coach somewhere. From there, it's only one more step to the pros.

That must have been the unstated dream of some of the men who volunteered to coach. My assistant was one of them.

I didn't know that at first, but it didn't take long to find out. It happened within ten minutes at our first practice.

After we finished checking to make sure everyone who had showed up was on our team, I sent the kids out into the field so we could judge how well they could catch. It was then my assistant made his first suggestion.

"Uh, Paul," George began, "don't you think we should have them warm up first, before we begin?"

Now forgetting for a moment the conflicting research about the benefits of stretching—some of the studies support the conventional wisdom that says stretching and mild aerobics in advance will reduce the chance of aches, sprains, and torn Achilles' tendons during a workout, while other data indicate all that huffing and puffing makes absolutely no difference— I have never met a six-, seven-, or eight-year-old who is in need of limbering up. While I may move like the Tin Man when I awake, Peter has been known to open his eyes and then do a somersault to get out of bed. (He's now on his third set of box springs.)

Still, asking if the kids should warm up was not a ridiculous question, and I had promised myself that I would be better about delegating.

"Hey, that's a good idea. Why don't you lead them?"
Big mistake.

George began by having them do jumping jacks—a hundred jumping jacks. From there it was push-ups (twenty-five), sit-ups (fifty), and running in place for three minutes.

While the kids were in the middle of doing "five laps around the field," I went over to George and asked if he thought the kids might be ready to go out and play some ball soon.

"You got to toughen them up, Paul," he said. "You don't want them letting us down when the game is on the line in the late innings."

Huh? Where did it say that I was going to have Knute Rockne as my assistant?

"First of all, George, we don't have late innings. We only play six. Second, these kids don't need a lot of conditioning."

And that was true. With the exception of Bobby Foley, who really was built like the proverbial fireplug, the other nine members of the team looked exactly like Peter—tall, skinny, and in perfect shape.

"But we have to toughen them up," said George.

"Why?"

Seeing that I clearly had no idea about the way things should be done, George volunteered to go work with the outfielders. But it wasn't any better over there. His idea of constructive criticism was to yell, "*No!*" every time a kid misjudged a fly ball (and believe me, it was far easier to keep track of the number they caught than the ones they missed). He dismissed most of the team as "hopeless" by the end of this our first practice.

In short, he was exactly the kind of coach I had been afraid Peter would get. But Peter wasn't stuck with him. I was.

This was not going to work.

When practice was over and the parents came back to pick up their kids, I walked George to his car.

"You know," I said, "I am probably not the right coach for you to be working with. I'm just not going to make the kids hit the ground and give me twenty pushups if they miss a fly ball or strike out. I just don't think that the games should be all that competitive at this level. Sure it would be nice to win some games, but I'm more concerned that the kids have a good time—and if they end up leaving here knowing more about baseball, I'll be thrilled and, to be honest with you, a little bit shocked."

George didn't disagree. It had to be clear to him that there was nothing I could do to advance his coaching career—if that indeed was what he had in mind. I never did find out for sure. He just could have been yet another overstressed executive who didn't know how to be anything other than hyperactive.

I offered to let him take his kid to another team—"trades" were not unheard of in situations like this—but he said no. We shook hands and George drove off. That was the last I saw of him. His wife brought their son to practice from then on.

As George drove away, I have to tell you that I was feeling pretty proud of myself. I had handled a potentially difficult situation well (he said humbly). Maybe I had hope as a manager after all.

But just as I was feeling like Robert Young in "Father Knows Best," a terrible feeling came over me. I no longer had an assistant coach.

That was no small thing. Just keeping tabs on eleven kids is hard enough, but if you want to spend some time doing one-on-one instruction—I was convinced I could teach Takeshi not to swing like Reggie Jackson; and at the very least I wanted Michael Goodman to stop flinching every time

34

the ball came within twenty feet of him—then you need at least one other person to watch and work with everyone else.

As I started walking off the field toward my car, I had no idea what I was going to do. Then Steve Moreno—who had spent the entire first practice watching from the sideline shouting encouragement to everyone, not just his son—solved my problem for me. As he was pulling out of the parking lot, he stopped by my car.

"They didn't look too bad," he said. "You should have a good year. Let me know if there's anything I can do to help."

I didn't hesitate a second. "You wanna be an assistant coach? George has made other plans."

Steve didn't hesitate either. He said yes. And on the ride home I had another thought. Other than Steve, the only parent I had been seriously worried about was Michael Roman's father, Frank, the sports fanatic. Even during the first workout, he had been taking notes on how well Michael was doing, charting where his hits were going (honest!), and constantly yelling out things like "Mikey, bend your knees."

There was nothing wrong with that, but I was concerned that he would become even more obsessive as the season continued. I figured I might be able to eliminate another potential problem if I drafted him to help out as well. After all, he knew the game, and if he was teaching Justin Marconi how to play shortstop, it would take some of the pressure off his son—and me. I called him later that night, he also said yes, and suddenly I had a staff.

I had coaches, a couple of kids who could play, and had even survived my first managerial test.

All right.

Let's play ball!

I should have controlled my enthusiasm.

6

Our First Exhibition Game: We Find Out How Good We Are (Hint: I Haven't Ordered Our World Series Rings Yet)

All our practices were pretty much the same. Takeshi kept pretending he was a combination of Jose Canseco and Mickey Mantle and continued to swing as hard as he could at anything near the plate. (Every once in a while he'd hit the ball straight up into the air.) Peter could be counted on to sweep in from center field to try to get every ground ball hit to an infielder, and Michael Goodman did everything in his power to avoid being any part of the action.

Oh, you could see some improvement. Stevie had stopped playing "toreador" defense (a famous technique—which is even practiced by many pros—where you wave at the ball as it goes by, instead of standing in front of it as you are supposed to do). Bobby Foley was picking up nuances of the game by the minute. During one of our base-running drills, he deliberately threw behind a runner who had made too big a turn at first, so the ball was waiting at the base when the runner tried desperately to scramble back. And Wei Yang continued to be solid in the field and at bat.

At the supermarket or at Science Day at school, when I ran into the other coaches (and they had stopped being Bill or Mike, but rather the manager who had Danny McGrath, clearly the best athlete in the league, or Julie Johnson, one of the league's three girls, each of whom was far better than anyone on our team) the conversation always went like this:

Danny McGrath's coach: "How does your team look?"

Me: "Okay, I guess. I don't think we are going to be embarrassed."

But the fact was I really didn't know for sure. For the most part, all we did twice a week was infield drills, where I'd hit the kids ground balls and say for the 237th time, "Keep your body in front of it." Then we worked on our hitting. "Michael, it will probably help a little bit if you keep your eyes open as the pitch heads toward the plate." But none of this told me how we'd do during a game.

We had played a two-inning "scrimmage" where we lost 13-8, but that didn't count for much. I deliberately put our worst hitters at the top of the lineup so they'd get more turns at bat, and I let the kids play any position they wanted. Peter, who figures he's on a par with Darryl Strawberry, the Los Angeles Dodgers $4-million-a-year-man, chose to play Darryl's position, right field, traditionally home to the worst fielder in Little League since very few balls are hit that way.

So I was telling the truth when I said I had no idea how good we were. Did everyone have a Michael Goodman on the team? Were three kids who knew how to play really enough to carry a team for a season?

I'd find out at our first exhibition game, which was scheduled during our third week of practice.

37

Some context: Remember, please, that first and second graders were playing in what was billed as an "instructional league." There were no league standings, no trophies for the team that finished first, no all-star team, and no most-valuable-player awards. (All those things were present in the higher grades.) Our games were just designed to teach kids a little bit about baseball, and to make sure that their first experience in organized sports didn't result in them writing *Coach Dearest* twenty-five years from now.

So why then were there exhibition games? If the *regular* games weren't going to mean anything, why would you bother holding *practice* ones?

I had already figured out the answer. The regular games would count. Oh, not in the same way they do in other sports. (For example, the chief financial officer of a *Fortune 500* company, who doubles as our basketball league president, mails out weekly team standings that he plots on a spread-sheet. In addition to giving the teams' cumulative record, he shows how far each team is behind the league leader, and what their record is versus every other team. He even provides each team's "average margin of victory" and a list of the league's top-ten scorers.)

But the fact was that the coaches, parents, and perhaps most important, the kids, were going to be tracking exactly how well they, and everyone else, did—even if they weren't supposed to. Hence, exhibition games.

We lost our first one. (That was the game where Justin tackled Peter on the final play.) But as the losing coaches have said since Abner Doubleday invented baseball, our first game "was a learning experience."

Specifically, I learned: *Parents are going to judge you on just two things.* In order of importance: One, how did you treat my kid, and two, did you win?

38

Both those things became clear from the very first pitch. While all the parents of our kids were, in theory, cheering for our team, just about all their attention was focused on their own child. That meant, I quickly discovered, I had to be very careful about what I said.

While general managerial instructions such as "Come on, guys, show more hustle," were fine, comments like "Michael, keep your body in front of the ball" as another one went zipping by Michael G. into left field, were not.

After being glared at by the Goodmans, you only heard positive things ("Nice try, Michael, but maybe next time you might want to think about . . .") coming out of my mouth for the rest of the season.

And if I still had any delusions that parents were not going to take these games seriously, they ended as soon as Justin tackled Peter.

As I walked back to my car, I heard parents second-guessing the way I had managed during the game. Specifically, they were questioning my decision to play different kids at different positions during the game.

I had decided on that strategy during draft night.

As far back as I can remember, which is probably the first time I played organized sports, I've always believed that putting a kid who can't catch out in right field for every inning of every game should be a capital offense. Even if you don't care what it did to the right fielder's ego—and everybody who was permanently banished to right field as a kid still carries some sort of emotional scar—think about what it says about you. You're telling the world: "Winning to me is *everything*. I'll go to any length, including embarrassing a seven-year-old, just to ensure that my team wins."

That might be fine if you are Vince Lombardi, Jr., but in the suburbs, it's just ridiculous. No kid in Holmdel is going to need an athletic scholarship to attend college, and as far back as anyone can remember no one from town ever went on to play pro anything. Given that, there was absolutely no reason to take the games seriously—and that was doubly true when you were talking about games involving kids who were six, seven, or eight years old.

So, my plan from the beginning was that everyone would play the infield for three innings and the outfield for three. (Remember, we only played six-inning games.) I wasn't as good about this as I could have been. I planned to hedge my bets. Since shortstop and center field tend to be two of the three most critical positions on the field (first base being the third), I intended to put one of the kids who could be counted on to catch the ball at short and center at all times. In the exhibition game, for example, Peter started at shortstop and moved to center field in the fourth inning, and Bobby Foley, who had been in center, moved to short.

This democratic approach was fine, my second-guessers seemed to be saying, providing my decision doesn't result in the wrong kid (Justin Marconi) being in the wrong place (left field) at the wrong time (when the game is on the line).

What was it that Al Davis, chairman of the Los Angeles, formerly world-champion Oakland, Raiders is fond of saying? Just win, baby?

7

A Funny Thing Happened on the Way to Our First Real Game: We Won (and a Lot of Parents Got Upset)

Our first real game was marked by four equally important occurrences.

1. Agam Chakavarty made his debut and in the tradition of 1930s Broadway musicals, he walked out onto the field an unknown and returned to the dugout a star. It was clear he was our best player.

2. We saw the beginning of my obsession with managing.

3. I found out that I didn't have parent-coach relations as much under control as I thought.

4. We won.

The last point proved to be relatively minor.

Let's take them from the top. Starting with my own version of Ruby Keeler—Agam Chakavarty.

About once a week after the season began, I'd call Agam's house to remind his parents when we had practice and to ask—again—if Agam would be able to make it. They'd assure me he'd be there but he never was. Agam was well on his way to becoming a pain in the backside in addition to being an enigma.

The fact that I didn't know much about him wasn't surprising. Nobody did. The general consensus was that he was smart (he was in all the "gifted and talented" programs at school and Holmdel has a lot of them) and his parents had money. His father is a cardiologist. But that's all I—and just about everybody else—knew. Could he play baseball? Would he play baseball? Who knew, and after the fourth phone call to his house, who cared?

There were rumors—Peter reported—that Agam really did want to play, but his father thought two practices and a game a week would take too much time away from his studies. In Holmdel, with its extremely competitive school system, parents of even first and second graders said that sort of thing all the time—and meant it.

Because of his father's reservations Agam had apparently talked his mother into signing him up for Little League, but neither Peter, nor anyone else, had ever seen him play baseball or any other organized sport.

If he didn't show up, I wasn't going to be crushed. I figured he'd be adequate at best and I didn't need adequate. I needed good.

The word on the grapevine was that Chris, the construction company owner, had four kids who could play, and that Mike Santiago had four, including two kids—if the stories could be believed—good enough to start for Holmdel High. Sure I was happy with Peter, Michael Roman, and Bobby, but I needed a superstar.

And that is what Agam turned out to be.

About halfway through the last practice before our season

began, a Lincoln Town Car pulled up along the third base foul line and a short, thin Indian child got out and came running toward me.

"Mr. Brown," he began, "my name is Agam Chakavarty and I would like to play."

"Fine," I said. "We're in the middle of infield drills. Go out to second base and I'll hit you some."

I always put our worst fielders at second. The throw to first is the shortest from there so even if they bobble (or mangle) a ground ball hit to them, they still have a chance of getting the runner out.

Agam trotted onto the field and immediately I began to feel better. When you tell 90 percent of first and second graders to go play second base, they immediately go stand on, or very near, second base. That makes sense. You told them to play second base, so where else should they go? If the third baseman stands near third, and the first baseman plays near first, logic tells you that the second baseman should be within a lunge or two of second.

But Agam knew that the second baseman plays between first and second, and that's exactly where he positioned himself.

As I did with all the kids when they took infield practice for the first time, I hit him five ground balls. The first went as slowly as I could hit it without having it stop all together, and I increased the speed with each swing. I hit the last one hard to Agam's right—the most difficult play for a second baseman since it requires him to reach across his body to make the play—but he fielded that one, as he had the four before it, cleanly.

Well, all right!

But what Agam did next convinced me that we had a true player on our hands.

As part of the infield drill, the third baseman, shortstop, and second baseman all throw the ball to first after they pick up the grounder. The first baseman makes the play himself. Once he fields the ball he races over and tags the base.

In the pros, of course, if the ball is hit far enough to the first baseman's right, the pitcher runs over to cover the bag. I had thought about having our "pitcher's helper"—a concept that is explained in the next chapter—make that play, but I figured the idea was too advanced for this level.

I tell you all this because of what happened next. Agam was playing between first and second, Michael Roman was playing first. I meant to hit the ball right to Michael but it sailed a bit too far toward second. Michael got to it, but if this had happened during a game there would have been no way he'd be able to beat the runner to first.

But that was okay, he wouldn't have had to. As Michael moved toward second to field the ball, Agam ran toward first to cover the base. Michael caught the ball and flipped it to Agam for what would have been an easy out. They exchanged high fives and both stared in at me with huge grins on their faces.

I was stunned. I hollered great play and figured it was a fluke. What Agam had done required an amazing understanding of the game. However, I couldn't help myself. Right before the infield drill was going to end, I hit the ball to the same spot. And again Michael got to it, and again Agam went over to cover first base.

As the kids jogged in to practice their hitting, I asked Agam if he had ever played shortstop and he said sure, "back in India." (It turns out he had gone to the American school over there.) I had him stay out in the field as each kid took five swings and he caught anything hit near him.

44

Given his fielding, it would have been asking too much to expect him to be able to hit, too, but of course he could. He had a short, compact swing that produced nothing but line drives. Baseball announcers like to say "he hit a rope," and I never knew what that meant before. But now I did. The balls that Agam hit looked as if they were attached to a rapidly moving clothesline suspended about twelve feet off the ground.

I had my fourth player and it was a good thing too. Because as I found as the first real game approached, this managing stuff was taking up more and more of my time.

It seemed like there was at least one coaches meeting a week, one to go over first aid, another to review the rules, that sort of thing. But that wasn't the real problem. What was taking up all my time—and I do mean *all* my time—was arranging potential batting orders and figuring out who was going to play where, when.

For example:

• Did I put all my best hitters up front and virtually concede that once we got to the lower part of the order, we'd go out one-two-three?

• But if I alternated good and weak hitters, wouldn't I be guaranteeing we'd never have a big inning? Two kids would get a hit, then there'd be an out. Two more hits, another out. That sort of thing.

• And what about positions? I was committed to having everybody play half the game in the infield and the other half in the outfield, but was it better to put my best fielder at shortstop for the first three innings or the last?

I knew spending *any* time on this was ridiculous. (Wasn't I the guy who swore he wasn't going to take any of this too seriously?) But here I was *constantly* shuffling eleven index cards—one card for each kid on the team. "Let's see, if I put Peter up first, then Takeshi, then I could . . ."

Now it wasn't as if I was doing this occasionally—say, during the odd moment on the 7:01 A.M. train out of Matawan to New York. Oh no, I was doing it all the time.

Instead of revising a magazine piece that was due in a couple of hours, I was revising—for the thirty-seventh time—my batting order.

Was I paying attention to my wife when she was telling me what needed to be fixed around the house? No. I was trying to figure out where I could put Michael Goodman so he would do the least damage when it was his turn to play in the infield.

I was thinking about this stuff in the shower, at the gym, and everywhere in between.

This was not good.

And like all people with personality disorders, I began to rationalize my problem away.

I'm becoming obsessive only because the first game is coming up, I told myself. (And because we had looked so awful during practice and the exhibition games.) I'll be better once the season is underway.

It's not a character flaw. Honest. I'm not turning into one of those sports-obsessed fathers. Really.

I'll be fine once we win our first game.

And, in fact, that happened immediately. We won game #1. It wasn't even close.

I had decided to bunch our best hitters at the top of the lineup, starting with the two or three kids I knew would get on base most of the time. Peter led off and hit the first pitch up the middle for what should have been a single. He ended up at third when the center fielder bobbled it and then threw it somewhere in the direction of first base. From there we never looked back. Agam hit a homer. Bobby hit two and even Michael Goodman managed to stop—if not catch—a ground ball hit right at him.

Final score, 29-4.

True, the opposition was awful. At one point their right fielder managed to throw the ball *backward*, and I don't think they hit one ball hard all day. (This team would end up winning exactly one game all season.) But hey, a win's a win and I was feeling pretty good—until the parents on my team started "congratulating" me.

"Paul, great game. The kids really looked good out there. But you're not really going to have (my kid) bat ninth (tenth or eleventh) all year are you?"

"Hey, great job. But on a couple of those close plays it looked like you were bending over backwards." I knew the play she was talking about. We were ahead by 20 at that point, and I called one of their poorer players safe on a not-so-close play at first.

"The kids looked like they were having fun out there, Coach. But, say, I was wondering if little Whoever (who hadn't yet caught a ball in practice) might get a chance to play shortstop in the next game or two?"

And so it went until I had gathered up all the equipment and stowed it in my trunk. The parents of the kids who played well were ready to make me manager of the year. If their kid didn't play well or they were "concerned" about where I had played him (or put him in the batting order), they felt obligated to mention it to me "in passing."

I went home, opened a beer as my celebratory gesture (I had thought about lighting up a cigar, à la the Boston Celtics' Red Auerbach, but cigars have always made me sick), and then started to figure out how I was going to make ten sets of parents happy.

I laid the index cards out on my desk, stared at them for a couple of seconds, and then said "Oh, the heck with it. We won!"

The second beer tasted even better than the first.

8

Reflections of a Manager with a Perfect (1-0) Record

In addition to relieving me of my fear of going 0-for-the-season, our first game introduced me to the vagaries of the rules governing baseball at this level, such as the one that required me to be the pitcher.

It didn't take me long to get used to the idea of pitching to my own kids. It even had a certain logic to it. The chances of finding a seven- or eight-year-old who could consistently throw strikes were about as good as me managing the Yankees. (Although after my stunning debut . . .) So, that meant having a coach pitch.

But which coach?

The question answered itself. You couldn't have the opposing coach pitch to the kids because the temptation to strike out one of them—to benefit his team—might prove too great.

So that left you with only one other choice: coaches had to pitch to their own kids.

But while the pitching rule made sense, there were others that defied understanding. And the more I tried to figure them out, the more perplexed I got.

For example:

This manager-as-umpire rule is a disaster waiting to happen. There was absolutely no way that having the coaches and managers double as umpires was going to work.

I understood the theory behind it. If the games don't count, why should the league spend money to hire umpires? True, it wouldn't cost very much. In the older grades (starting at the third- and fourth-grade level), high-school kids were paid $25 a game to officiate. But since this is just the instructional league, the thinking goes, why pay anything at all?

Why? Because it is quite likely that I'm going to be a victim every time.

On a close play, my first inclination was to make the call *against* our team. If there was *any* doubt, I would call our kids out and the other team's safe.

My sense of fair play was fine, except:

1. It meant, by definition, that I would be cheating our team out of half the legitimate calls it should get. (After all, the odds say that half of those close calls should go our way.)

2. My kids will think my approach to umpiring is the dumbest thing they've ever heard of. They don't want *any* calls to go against them. (They screamed and yelled on close plays during intrasquad games, for Pete's sake. They sure weren't going to be thrilled when their own coach "turned" on them during real games and started making calls that would benefit the other side.)

3. And most important of all, according to the parents of my kids, there is absolutely no guarantee that my trying to be a nice guy is going to be reciprocated.

Obviously, if I bend over backward to call things your way when I'm umpiring, I'm going to hope you return the favor when your kids are up at bat. (The coach who is pitching to his kids makes all the calls during that half inning.)

However, as two of the parents on my team were quick to point out, after I called Bobby Foley out in game one on a close play where it was clear to everyone—including me—that he was probably safe, the odds of that happening were not great.

They were proven right in the very next inning. On a play that was almost identical to the one that involved Bobby, the opposing coach called his kid safe.

"Did you see that?" several parents asked me at once. "They're just going to take advantage of you." For what's it's worth, we were ahead 23-3 at the time. Whatever happened to the games just being in fun?

The "ninth batter" rule. We've already touched on part of this. Without the rule, given the level of defense, it would be possible for one team to be at bat for thirty or forty minutes at a time. With the games starting somewhere between 5:30 and 6:00 P.M., letting each team hit until there are three outs is probably not the best idea. Having six-, seven-, and eight-year-olds coming home at two and three in the morning—the time the games would probably end—would do little to foster learning the next day.

To get around this problem, some leagues call off games when they get out of hand—say, when one team gets ahead by 12 runs.

Others employ a variation of what we did as kids when we

played Ping-Pong. If you score a certain number of runs, somewhere between 7 and 10, before the other team gets any, you automatically win.

Our version was more complicated: in any given inning, no more than nine kids could hit.

Let's take the first inning as an example to show how this works.

Suppose after the first eight kids have hit, the situation looks like this: You've already scored 4 runs, the bases are loaded, there's one out, and the ninth batter is coming up.

Here's what happens:

First, everybody—coaches, parents, the guy in the ice cream truck parked outside the foul line—screams "Ninth batter, ninth batter!" in an attempt to remind the kids what is about to happen.

It doesn't help. Invariably, the kid who'll end up fielding the ball either forgets what he is supposed to do or just stands there—ball firmly in hand—because he doesn't know *what* he's supposed to do. And in his defense, there are an awful lot of options.

If the ball is caught in the air, the batter is out and the inning is over.

If it's hit on the ground to the infield, you can throw the ball to first, and if the ball gets there before the runner does, the inning is over.

The same holds true if the fielder tries to get a force play at any base. As long as the ball beats the runner to the base, the runner is out and the inning is over.

So, in other words, on routine plays even when the ninth batter is up, the easiest thing to do is pretend everything is normal and play "regular" baseball.

There are, alas, a couple of exceptions.

Consider what happens if the batter gets a base hit, or the ball arrives too late to get the runner at first, or at any other, base. The game quickly begins to resemble not baseball but a Chinese fire drill.

In either of those situations, someone must be holding the ball while standing on home plate in order to end the inning.

The easiest thing to do, of course, is have whoever fields the ball throw it home to the catcher.

Simple?

Yes.

Effective?

No.

Given the general accuracy of a seven-year-old's throws, there is absolutely no guarantee that the ball would come anywhere near home plate. And even if it did, the odds of it being caught are remote at best.

Since there is no stealing in this league, and no passed balls or wild pitches (how could there be, the coaches do all the pitching?), teams tend to play their worst kids at catcher. In fact, I usually played without a catcher at all. It was just too burdensome to keep helping the catcher on and off with his equipment at the end of each inning.

So, not surprisingly, most coaches tell their kids, "No matter where you are when the ninth batter is up, if the ball is hit to you, just pick it up and run home."

Now, since the batter—and anyone on base—will be running around the bases while the fielder is sprinting home (if a base runner makes it home before an out is recorded or the ball gets there, the run counts), collisions and confusion are inevitable.

It's fun to watch, but I'm not really sure what it has to do with baseball.

Pitcher's Helper. Since the coaches pitch to their own kids, you have to figure out what to do on ground balls hit back to the pitcher.

You could, I suppose, have the coach field the ball, but that would lead to all kinds of problems. For one thing, the kids would hate it. It would mean their coach, in essence, would be playing against them.

Then there'd be the question of what would happen if the coach made a *legitimate* error—he muffed the catch or made a bad throw. The chances of that happening once or twice a game were pretty good. With the average age of the coaches being on the far side of thirty-five, hand/eye coordination was usually lacking.

And we won't even raise the possibility of a coach making a deliberate error to help his team. This is, after all, an instructional league, and who would even think about doing that?

If the coach *did* make an error, even a legitimate one, it would appear he was trying to give his own team a break. Screaming, yelling, and general temper tantrums—by both parents and kids—would follow.

The solution was to create the "pitcher's helper," a defensive player who would stand next to the coach and field anything hit his way.

An aside. Since the coaches in Little League stand about thirty feet away from the batter when they pitch, we required the pitcher's helper to wear a batting helmet, complete with clear plastic face mask, just in case he didn't react fast enough on a ball hit right at him.

That was fine, of course, but no one thought of providing protection for the coach doing the pitching, and there is no doubt in my mind that a seven-year-old, even one who doesn't understand baseball very well, is going to react far faster to a batted ball than some thirty-seven-year-old, out-of-shape executive who was not all that well coordinated to begin with.

During the season, you could count on each coach being hit by at least one batted ball. The most vicious hit came off the bat of Freddie Peruggia, one of the best hitters in the league, who hit his coach squarely on the nose with a line drive, breaking his glasses with a "snap" that could be heard on the other side of the field. (The coach, who fell to the ground after being hit, escaped with just a bloody nose.)

There was plenty of talk about requiring the coaches to wear a jock and cup while they pitched—we made the kids do it—but it never became mandatory. Even in middle age, it seems the desire to be macho dies hard.

There were two schools of thought about pitcher's helpers. Some coaches, me included, put their worst fielders on the mound. Our feeling was that if the pitcher's helper missed the ball, it was no big deal; you still had the infielders (and the outfielders) to back up the play. I believed this so strongly that I wouldn't even use a pitcher's helper if we were short of players. More on that in a second.

But other coaches put their best fielders on, or slightly behind, the pitcher's mound. Their thinking was their most talented kid should get first crack at catching everything. Since the ball was rarely hit hard, whoever stood in the center of the infield had an excellent chance of making every play. The pitcher's helper rule—like everything else—was destined to be a point of controversy.

Everybody plays all the time. This was the hardest regulation to get used to. In all other sports the township offered, the general rule-of-thumb was that everybody had to play at least half the game. You played with the regulation five players in basketball, for example, and made sure that all nine players on your team got in for half the game.

But we were in an instructional baseball league, and the best way to learn—as the old saw goes—is by doing. So everybody would play all the time. That led to some interesting decisions.

"Okay, here's the batting order: Peter, first; Takeshi, second; . . . Wei, tenth; Michael Goodman, eleventh . . ."

But as strange as that sounds—and, believe me, telling someone he's batting eleventh sounds pretty strange—finding positions for everyone proved even weirder.

You start with the basics, of course: first base, second base, third, short, and three outfielders—left, center, and right. But that only accounts for seven of your eleven players. A pitcher's helper would be eight. And I always put a kid right on second base. But that still left me with two kids unaccounted for.

My solution was to put them in the outfield. One kid would play left field near the foul line—to the right of the left fielder. (See, I told you this would sound strange.) Another would play right center.

But if you could play with eleven, you could also play with less. The rule was whoever showed up played. And there were days—thanks to kids being out with colds or on vacations with their parents—that you'd have less than a full complement. We played with as many as eleven and as few as seven (no catcher, no pitcher's helper). Heck, there were even two games we played with nine.

For the opening game everybody showed up and by the fourth inning or so, I got used to saying things like "Stevie, go to left center; Tommy, I want you at pitcher's helper for the next couple of innings."

It sounded odd, but what the heck. It was baseball. Sort of.

9

Game #2: Boy, Can You Get Overconfident in a Hurry

For the first time since I signed up to coach, I approached game #2 with the right attitude.

I figured there was no pressure. Having won our first game, the worst that could happen was that we'd lose this one. That would make our record 1-1, and that would be just fine. I would be *thrilled* to have a .500 season. Anything less than that would be embarrassing. Losing them *all* would have been humiliating.

Finishing above .500 would be nice, but since I didn't expect it to happen, it wasn't something I had thought about a lot. Half and half was about what I was expecting, and there was no way that I could come out of this game with a record that was worse than that.

So I went into game #2 in the perfect frame of mind, and

it was this relaxed, hey-isn't-this-fun attitude that got us into trouble.

But not immediately.

We were up first, and my hours of shuffling index cards had apparently paid off. My lineup looked like this:

1. Peter
2. Takeshi
3. Agam
4. Michael Roman
5. Bobby
6. Stevie
7. Tommy
8. Wei Yang
9. John
10. Michael Goodman
11. Justin

And it was, he said humbly, a pretty good batting order. Peter could always be counted on to get on base. He hit the ball hard, and since there were just a handful of kids you could call good fielders, that alone was enough to guarantee a hit. As Peter told anyone who asked—and a lot of people who didn't—he batted .800 for the season, or about twice what Ted Williams, perhaps the greatest hitter in baseball history, recorded in his best year.

While an .800 batting average was impressive, in this league it was far from unique. About the only time you could get even a mediocre hitter out, given the general level of defense, was when one of the fielders caught the ball in self-defense. Peter's experience was typical. A couple of times his balls were caught when someone put his glove up to protect his face and the ball stuck in the webbing.

But for the most part Peter always led off the game by getting on base. He'd tell you that they were all scorching singles up the middle or wicked line drives in the right center or left center field alleys. However, the truth was that the ball probably bounced off someone's glove. But no matter how it happened, Peter got on base about eight times out of ten.

And he ended up on first leading off this game as well. Peter hit a (legitimate) single up the middle, and up to the plate stepped Takeshi, who, by the day, was becoming more American than a farm kid from Iowa.

Not only had he mastered English—with no accent—he also had American slang down. "I'm batting second and playing second, right?" he asked me before the game. When I said yes, he said, "All right!" I figured any day now he'd start wearing clothes in neon colors—electric lime-green pants, neon purple shirts, and the like had just become all the rage with the preteen set.

Along with Takeshi's total Americanization had come an uneasy truce with the art of hitting. I had spent a lot of time explaining that it wasn't necessary for him to swing as hard as he could on every pitch. Sure, home runs were nice, I said, but we needed people to get on base, too. Besides, hadn't he noticed how few home runs were actually hit during "real" baseball games? My beloved 1961 Yankees hold the record for the most home runs in a single season—240—but even that works out to only 1.5 homers a game.

"So, Takeshi, you can see how important it is for people to hit singles and doubles, right?"

Takeshi would listen to this very intently, nod at all the right places, and promise that from now on all he was going to try to do was meet the pitch. Then he'd see Agam or Bobby Foley whack the hell out of the ball, jog around the bases,

59

and get high fives from their teammates for hitting a home run and he'd go up to the plate and start swinging from his heels again.

We—actually, Takeshi did it all by himself—finally worked out a compromise. On the first pitch, he'd swing as hard as he could. Invariably, he'd miss. From then on he was very patient. The pitch had to be absolutely perfect. (Since the coaches pitch, there are no balls or strikes so a hitter can stand up at the plate all day.) When he finally got a pitch to his liking, generally waist-high over the exact middle of the plate, he'd smile and deliver a swing that could be used in a Little League training film. His eyes stayed on the ball the whole time, his bat remained perfectly level, and he'd aim for the exact center of the ball.

And invariably that's exactly where he hit it. If the bat hits the bottom of the ball, it goes up. If you top the ball, it goes down, and hitting it in the middle—as Takeshi almost always did—produces a line drive that is rarely caught by first or second graders.

So we began this game, as we usually did, with Peter on second, Takeshi on first, and Agam, Michael Roman, and Bobby Foley coming up. I could count on at least one of them hitting a home run, even on our worst days. Since this was one of our better ones, they all did. Suddenly it was 5-0, and there was still nobody out. We were off to a good start.

And it stayed that way through the first couple of innings. We scored 6 in the first, 2 in the second, 7 in the third (as the top of the order came around again). As we began the fourth inning we were ahead, 15-2. It was then that I just got plain stupid. I decided to show off.

Figuring the game was well in hand, I called my kids over and asked them if they wanted to try something new. I'd pitch overhand to anyone who wanted me to. But I didn't stop there.

I also said, "When we go back on the field in the bottom of the fourth, you can play any position you want to."

Let's take each of these asinine decisions one at a time.

While league rules didn't require you to pitch underhand, all the coaches did. Why? First, your control is better. (Don't believe it? Stand ten feet away from a wastepaper basket. Try to throw ten pieces of crumpled-up paper into the basket underhand, then throw another ten in overhand. You make more baskets the first way. Guaranteed.)

The second reason for pitching underhand is that it's less threatening to kids. They know you can't throw the ball hard that way, plus it's easier for them to see it. When you throw underhand, you hold the ball out in front of you the entire time. When you pitch overhand, the ball becomes obscured for a split second as you bring your arm back.

Given all this, it wasn't surprising that everybody pitched underhand.

But, as the second graders already knew, the rules would change for them next year. In the third and fourth grades, not only did the kids—not the coaches—pitch, they pitched overhand. Since all second graders want to be third graders—*today*!—they jumped at the chance to hit overhand pitching, just like the "big" kids did.

The problem was they couldn't do it. At least not well. So when I pitched overhand in the top of the fourth, we scored exactly 2 runs. Okay, I said, no big deal. We were still ahead, 17-2.

But then I promptly compounded my mistake.

With the game clearly out of reach, I figured this was my chance to answer all those parents who'd asked when their kid was going to get a chance to play a key position on defense. The answer was, "Right now."

In the bottom of the fourth, I moved Peter from shortstop

to right field. (He was thrilled. It finally gave him the chance to pretend he was Darryl Strawberry in a real game.) I moved Agam from center to left, and in the most daring decision of all, I moved Michael Roman, who could have been nicknamed "Mr. Machine" for his ability to catch everything that was thrown anywhere near him at first base, and put him in left center.

With those three simple moves, I had managed to create a defensive scheme that made it unlikely that we'd be able to catch a thing.

And we didn't.

We promptly gave up 9 runs in the bottom of the fourth. What was particularly painful was that we should have gotten them out one, two, three. The first batter hit a ground ball to short, which either Agam or Peter could have fielded easily, but Agam or Peter wasn't there. Stevie was and he promptly used his glove as a cape, and the slow-charging bull of a ball ended up out in left.

The three ground balls that we did manage to field still resulted in base runners when the first baseman dropped each of the throws. It would be a long time before Michael Goodman played first again.

And so it went.

At the end of four, we led 17-11.

Now, if I were a rational human being, I would have called the inning an experiment and promptly gone back to our old alignment.

But no one was going to call me a "rational human being" and get away with it. I steadfastly continued to pitch overhand to the second graders in the top of the fifth, and this time we didn't score at all. We headed into the bottom half of the inning still ahead by 6.

This, of course, was the perfect time to go back to our old

defensive setup, but there wasn't a chance I was going to. *That* would have made sense. Agam stayed in left, Michael Roman was firmly planted in short left center, and Bobby and Peter spent the entire time chatting away in right center and right. We promptly gave up 6 more runs, and were only saved from total disaster when their best hitter connected on a ball that must have traveled 200 feet, right to Agam, who apparently was trying to set a record for deepest left field ever played by a second grader.

The score was tied, 17-17, at the end of five.

Having blown a 15-run lead as a direct result of lousy managing (as several of my players were quick to point out), the kids wanted no more of this pitching overhand stuff. And once I began throwing the way *I* used to, the kids began hitting the way *they* used to.

Justin led off our half of the sixth with a single; Peter singled. Takeshi hit a soft ground ball up the middle that the kid playing second caught, forcing Peter. Agam doubled, scoring Justin, Michael Roman singled Takeshi home, and Bobby Foley homered. We scored a total of 5, and took the field in the bottom of the sixth—and last—inning defending a 5-run lead.

I'd like to say that I stuck to my guns and kept all our fielders where they had been in the fourth and fifth innings. I'd like to say that I was going to use this game as an exercise in building character, and would show the world that I was taking the "instructional" part of the instructional league seriously. I'd like to say all that, but the plain fact was I didn't do any of those things. I choked.

"First inning positions," I yelled as everyone headed onto the field. That meant, of course, that I had my best fielders back in the key positions and the inning went pretty much as it was supposed to.

Pretty much. They scored 2 runs right away, then we caught two line drives, and then they singled twice, bringing the potential tying run to the plate.

The kid swung and hit the ball what seemed like a mile—straight up. It was destined to come down somewhere near the pitcher's mound.

"*Peter!!!!!!!!!!!!*" I yelled.

Peter, bless his little heart, as-calm-as-you-please, called, "I got it," and started drifting in from shortstop. He caught it, one-handed no less, and we won.

But I didn't feel particularly good about it.

10

Coaching Your Kid

For most of the kids on the team, knowing what to call me was a problem. "Mr. Brown" was a possibility, but when you're almost a teenager—as any six-, seven-, or eight-year-old will tell you that they are—"Mr. Brown" is seriously uncool.

"Paul" was a possibility but that suggested that we were peers, and there was no way anyone of an advanced age (thirty-five) could be considered a peer. A contemporary of their grandfathers perhaps, but not *their* peer. Anyone over sixteen, the average age of the New Kids on the Block, was officially considered old. And if you didn't know who the New Kids were (a bubble gum rock band popular with the under-eight set), you were beyond old. You were ancient.

"Coach" was kind of cool and some of the kids—Bobby Foley chief among them—preferred that form of address.

However, most of the kids just avoided calling me anything. Most, but not all.

"Dad, when are we . . ."

"Dad, watch this . . ."

"Dad, how come you . . ."

And Peter's dealings with me would remain different from the other kids throughout the season.

At first he figured he knew what the relationship would be: coach and assistant coach. After all, Peter reasoned, since he was ready to start for the Oakland A's tomorrow—neither my son nor daughter has ever been cursed with self-doubt—clearly he was also ready to run a Little League club as well. And while I, due to my advanced years ("Dad, *you* don't know who the New Kids are?"), would probably be in charge, Peter was clearly destined to be my number-one assistant. At least according to Peter. Inadvertently, I did little—at first—to squash the fantasy.

In the early part of the season, I made the mistake of discussing strategy with Peter, as I planned what I would do at upcoming games or practices. That was fine, except when I got up before the kids and said, "Today we're going to work on fundamentals, and—" Peter would rush in and finish the thought with, "—and we're also going to go over hitting the cutoff man, and work on how to cut the corners when we run the bases."

He knew what I was going to say—after all, I had gone over it with him ahead of time—and he felt compelled, as my assistant, to say it for me.

Telling him not to interrupt didn't seem to work, and neither did making him pledge not to reveal what I planned to talk about at practice. When you're seven, it's awfully hard to keep a secret. I finally stopped telling him anything at all ahead of time. He learned what we were going to do when the rest of the team did.

But that was the easy part. What was hard was trying to figure out how to deal with him during practices, scrimmages, and games.

The problem was twofold: Peter himself and the potential concerns of the parents of Peter's teammates. In a nutshell, they wanted to be sure that I wouldn't be favoring my son over theirs.

Peter proved to be the easier of the two problems. And he wasn't particularly easy.

When you aren't lacking in self-confidence, taking instruction can be difficult. After all, if you're fully prepared to be the starting left fielder for Oakland tomorrow should Rickey Henderson get hurt or go into one of his periodic sulks, why should you be willing to listen to what anyone—much less your father, a man who was old enough to have seen Mickey Mantle play—says about how you should hit, or field, or throw?

That was the bad news. The good news was that Peter has been this way since birth—in fact, since before birth. (Peter was so confident that he could handle the world, he was premature, showing up a full month early.)

Since I knew how Peter was with everything else ("I can do it, I can do it!" *Crash!* "How do you do it?"), I had a pretty good idea of how to handle him in baseball. I couldn't tell him anything—because he already knew it all—so the trick was to prove to him that what I was saying was true.

Here's an example. Like all kids, Peter has baseball heroes, and like all kids, he would copy everything they'd do. And while he loved Darryl Strawberry, for some reason Peter fell in love with Mel Hall, a journeyman outfielder who now plays for the Yankees. Hall is probably best remembered—if he is remembered at all—for having a few good years for Cleveland in the mid-1980s, where he consistently hit about .280 with between 15 and 18 home runs.

One thing that's unique about Hall is the way he holds his bat. Instead of keeping it slightly below his shoulders while waiting for the pitch, as most hitters do, Hall usually holds his bat chin-high. In profile he looks as if he has a chimney attached to his head.

Now batters make adjustments to their swings all the time and the results are often bizarre. Mel Ott, a Hall of Fame slugger who hit 521 home runs during his career, used to lift one foot off the ground before he swung, and Kevin Maas, the Yankees' current designated superstar, virtually faces right field when he bats. They adopted these strange positions in an attempt to correct some hitting flaw, and it's fair to assume that the same was true for Hall. Maybe he was having trouble with the high pitch at one point in his career and this weird stance was a way of compensating. It must have worked. Hall is a .276 lifetime hitter, productive enough for the Yankees to pay him over $1 million a year for part-time employment. (Until recently, Hall, a left-handed hitter, rarely played against left-handed pitching.)

But the problem with Hall's swing is that it makes it almost impossible to hit an inside pitch, especially one thrown low and inside, unless you have the reflexes of a pro athlete.

I told that to Peter. However, just telling Peter anything does no good. ("Don't worry, I can hit it, Dad, no matter where it is.") You have to show him. And so we would go out in the backyard and I'd throw dozens of pitches inside—low and inside and high and inside—and Peter, who almost always made contact with the ball when he batted with a "normal" stance, would miss each and every one.

That still wasn't enough. Invariably, he'd accuse me (and rightly so) of deliberately trying to throw pitches that he couldn't hit. I'd try to explain that during a game, a "real" game where pitchers could throw anywhere they wanted (which, of course, was exactly what would happen when he started playing in the third- and fourth-grade league), there'd be no guarantee that they wouldn't end up pitching him inside. In fact, that's exactly where they would pitch him, once they saw his stance.

I suggested that he lower his bat just a little and see what happened. He did, reluctantly. And all of a sudden he was hitting line drives all over the place, no matter where I threw the ball. After hitting twelve in a row either off the house or onto the roof, Peter smiled—also reluctantly—and agreed to *think* about modifying his stance.

With hitting taken care of, we moved on to fielding ground balls and the battle would start over again. "But why do I have to catch it with two hands? None of the pros do, and besides, I can do it perfectly this way, Dad, and . . ."

But in retrospect, Peter was easy compared to the parents. They kept watching to see if I'd favor Peter at the expense of everyone else.

Their fear was not irrational. Some background will help.

As a rule, the men who volunteer to coach any of the three sports Holmdel offers (soccer, basketball, and baseball) played some kind of organized ball as a kid: on "Y" teams, in high school, that sort of thing. We've even had former college athletes among our ranks. (The first time I coached—as an assistant, fortunately for all involved—I was helping out a guy who had captained the Dartmouth soccer team. It couldn't have been a better pairing. I hadn't played soccer since I was eight, and even then I didn't know what I was doing.)

If you played ball in high school or beyond, you had to be pretty good, and the odds say your kid is going to get some of your athletic genes.

Plus, if you were a jock in school, you probably liked playing sports and so you're bound to want your son to have the same experience.

All this means you're probably willing to spend hours in the backyard with your kid playing one-on-one or kicking a soccer ball into a net, sharing the tips you got and learned over the years.

The combination of good genes, coupled with lots of practice and one-on-one coaching, invariably results in all the plays being designed for the coach's kid. After all, he's almost always the best athlete on the team.

Almost always.

Peter, alas, couldn't claim that distinction. Agam and maybe even Bobby were probably better. Part of the problem was genetic. At 5'11" and 175 pounds, I couldn't be said to have the perfect athletic build. Average? Yes. Jose Canseco–like? No.

Then there was the simple fact that I never played baseball on a competitive level. In summer camp, after school, and in pickup games around the neighborhood? Sure. But never in high school. The baseball team played and practiced when the tennis team did. So the only strategy I learned came from watching hundreds of Yankee games as a kid. You can pick up some things that way—never make the first or last out of an inning being thrown out at third; try to get guys like Roger Maris and Mickey Mantle in your lineup, if you can—but it's not quite the same as playing Double-A ball in the Dodger organization, as one of the coaches did.

In addition to lacking in strategy, I was also shaky in the fundamentals. I knew enough to tell the kids to keep their body in front of the ball and to use two hands when making a catch, but after that things got awfully fuzzy.

So all this put Peter—and his teammates—at a substantial disadvantage. Peter, thanks to his genetics, was not the best player on our team, let alone in the league, and his father was nowhere near being the second coming of legendary manager John McGraw.

Still, none of the parents knew that as the season began. All they saw was this kid with freckles and a gap between his front teeth who was calling the coach "Dad" and who seemed to be getting preferential treatment. After all, he was usually playing shortstop and batting first.

This had all the makings of a major problem. But fortunately, Peter solved it for me simply by being Peter.

One of the things all the parents picked up on right away was the fact that I was rotating kids around to all positions. So while it was true that Peter sometimes played shortstop, he could also be found in the outfield—occasionally even in right field, as my ill-fated attempt at total democracy showed. The batting order, too, seemed to change from practice to practice as well.

But the biggest thing that worked in my favor was Peter's enthusiasm. He was always running, always diving—especially when he didn't have to—after balls. Then he'd make sure the entire world noticed his efforts, by either jumping up in the air, holding the ball straight above his head, or lying on the ground feigning an injury. If he wasn't absolutely filthy by the time a practice was over, we knew he was coming down with something.

It's hard to hate a seven-year-old extrovert, especially one who is clearly having as much fun as Peter was out on the field and up at bat.

Fortunately for me, most of the time Peter made the play,

which helped keep the parents off my back, as did the fact that I treated him the same as everyone else. If anything, I was quicker to criticize him. But even with the way I treated Peter, there was no reason to think there would be long-lasting emotional scars. "Peter, call for the ball," and "Make sure you touch all the bases," were about as strict as I got.

All this helped.

As did the fact that so far at least, we hadn't lost.

11

Game #3: Mothers. Sigh

Game #3 ended in a tie and almost in a fistfight. I was glad blows weren't exchanged because it would have been pretty embarrassing for me to have been beaten up by somebody's mother, and there's an excellent chance that's what would have happened. Some of the women out there made Jane Fonda look like Roseanne Barr.

As I've said, I knew from the beginning that parents could be a problem. After all, most of the Vince Lombardi/Killer Coaches—the kind who were fond of saying "It's not if you win or lose, it's if you win"—were parents. And I was worried about how they—and the other parents—would react if we went out and lost every game, or if their son didn't bat fourth and play shortstop.

But in all my worrying, I forgot one thing. The parents weren't going to be dissecting my performance from afar.

They'd be at every game. Some stayed for every practice as well. And, as I quickly found out, parents could be vicious. Especially the mothers.

To this day, I am not sure why the mothers gave me and every other coach such a hard time.

You can offer just about any theory you want.

In a lot of ways, Holmdel is a throwback to "The Donna Reed Show"/"Father Knows Best" suburbs of the 1950s and '60s. A surprisingly high percentage—well over half I'd guess—of the mothers don't work outside the home. In that kind of environment, some women tend to live their lives, and derive their sense of self-worth, through their husbands and children. Therefore they saw any slight to their kid, real or imagined, as an attack against them. And lack of quality playing time, or losing a Little League game that involved her son—her son who was clearly destined to become a Rhodes scholar and professional athlete—definitely qualified as a slight.

On a related note, the men in town tend to be among the most competitive on the planet. They would have to be, given what they've achieved. You don't build a $25-million construction company from scratch by being "laid back." And you don't earn your Ph.D. in applied astrophysics by not "sweating the details." It's only natural the women that they'd be attracted to would have similar personalities.

Then again, the fierceness could be nothing more than a mother's natural instinct to protect her young.

Even my wife, who by any objective measure would be judged to be the world's most levelheaded human being, is not immune when it comes to sports. Fortunately for me— and our son and daughter—she only becomes obsessed when it comes to swimming.

Anne Christine Peck can see Peter score the winning run in baseball or miss a critical shot in basketball, and her expression won't change. Afterward she will be just as calm and praise Peter's performance if he has a good day and be supportive if he doesn't.

But when it comes to swimming, all bets are off. She has seen Peter in dozens of races and yelled herself hoarse during each and every one of them.

You know how during the Olympics the networks go out of their way to keep a camera trained on the parents of some of the athletes who are competing? Well, I keep having this dream. It's the year 2004 and Peter is swimming for the Gold Medal in the backstroke in the summer Olympics, which are being held in someplace like Portugal. The camera alternates between a shot of Peter—who is in an extremely close race for first—and my wife, who is going certifiably nuts. My wife who *never* raises her voice is screaming her head off and pumping her fist—which more than likely is holding an American flag—in the air.

Ms. Peck has no explanation for her behavior. It can't be genetic. Her parents are soft-spoken and rational. And you can't blame the environment either. She grew up and attended college in Missouri, a good 1,200 miles from the nearest ocean. Similarly, she couldn't explain when I asked her why the mothers—many of whom she knew—kept giving me and every other coach a hard time.

Now, you have already figured out that I was not going to win "Mr. Calm, Cool, and Collected" for my performance during the season. And most of the fathers who watched our games were more emotional than I expected. Still, it was always the mothers who jeered loudest at calls they didn't like (which were being made by the coach/umpires, remember), who cheered loudest after a victory, and who were most inclined to bend the rules when it suited their needs. And that is exactly what happened in game #3.

It was a typical game, which meant the score was tied 21-21 at the end of four. What made the game slightly atypical was that it was taking longer than usual. This was just one of those days when it seemed each kid hit two or three foul balls every time he went up to bat, and just about everyone seemed to be taking more pitches than usual.

One of the downsides of not having a real umpire is that there is no way to call balls and strikes. Nobody, after all, is going to call a kid on his own team out on strikes. Some of these kids have enough problems hitting a ball when it's thrown perfectly, let alone worrying about whether somebody is going to call a borderline pitch that they didn't swing at a strike.

Conversely, there's no way the coach, since he's pitching to his own kids, can call anything a ball. Just think of the temptation of (deliberately?) walking your worst hitter to avoid having him strike out.

But without an umpire to keep the game moving, occasionally a kid would take the old baseball adage of "wait for a good pitch" literally. He'd stand up at the plate and look at maybe ten or fifteen pitches before he'd swing.

And on top of the combined 42 runs we had scored, all the foul balls, and kids waiting for the perfect pitch (and asking any of the coaches to consistently throw good pitches was asking an awful lot of middle-aged men, especially as the game went on and our unconditioned arms got tired), we had started late. No surprise there.

When you have four coaches (each team has at least one assistant, in addition to the manager), somebody is bound to be delayed coming from work. In addition, the other coaches and I were not above a little stalling before throwing out the first pitch, in the hope that one or two of our stars, who were not yet present, might still show up. Attendance wasn't mandatory and anything from CCD (Confraternity of Christian Doctrine religious education class) or Hebrew school to an excessive amount of homework could keep a kid away.

The net result of all this? The sun started to set during the bottom of the fourth.

Holmdel doesn't have lights on its Little League fields, so it's left to the coaches to decide when to call a game on account of darkness. Since the score was tied and the sun was going down, I figured this was as good a time as any to end the game. I went over to the other coach, Dan, who is a genuinely nice guy.

"You want to call it?" I asked.

"You know, it wouldn't be a bad idea," he said. "It would end in a tie and we could all go home happy."

"Fine."

The problem was that neither one of us had bothered to check with our kids. And it *wasn't* fine with them.

To an eight-year-old, the idea of ending a game before the final out is recorded is right up there with canceling Halloween. It's a seriously bad idea.

Kids haven't changed since the beginning of time. Given a choice between risking life and limb by trying to hit and catch a baseball in virtual darkness, or going home to have dinner (complete with vegetables and the obligatory glass of milk), and then inevitably being forced to do homework and go to bed, they will do anything—including wearing miners' helmets—to keep playing.

"You can't call the game!" I was told when I announced what Dan and I had decided to do.

"It's not dark!"

"It's not going to be really dark for another hour."

"I can see fine, honest."

Etc., etc.

Given the unanimous lack of support, Dan and I agreed to keep playing. "But we're not promising that we're going to let you finish the game," we both told our teams. "If it really looks like someone is going to get hurt out there, we're going to call it off."

But even that equivocation was enough to get us back in the kids' good graces. The game continued. Dan's team scored 3 in the top of the fifth, we answered with 4. And then they scored 2 more in the top of the sixth to reclaim the lead, 26-25.

By now it really was getting dark. Street lights were on, and all the cars that passed the field had their lights on as well. Still, the game was almost done and Dan and I figured we might as well finish it if we could.

The mothers on his team had other ideas.

As we were coming up in the bottom of the sixth, I got to meet some of them up close and personal, as they are fond of saying at ABC Sports. While they were attractive women individually, collectively they were not a pretty sight.

"You have to call the game," they said.

"The kids are going to get hurt," they said.

"You have to end the game right this second," they said.

"This is ridiculous," they said. "Call the game."

All these women were the mothers of the kids on Dan's team, but my buddy Dan was nowhere to be seen.

I tried to explain that Dan and I had wanted to end the game earlier, but the kids wouldn't let us. Since we'd agreed to let the kids keep playing and we had already come this far, it only seemed fair to play out the bottom of the sixth—and last—inning.

But the mothers—and curiously, all the fathers of the kids on Dan's team had chosen this exact moment to go for a walk—didn't want to hear about fairness or anything else. They wanted the game ended immediately.

If it did, of course, they'd win 25-24.

I wasn't about to let that happen. Why? Well, in part, because I am as competitive as the next guy. But more important was the fact that the mothers on Dan's team were starting to annoy me.

There had been no talk about ending the game for safety's sake when they were losing. But now, when they saw an easy chance to get a win (in their defense they had lost their first two games), continuing the game was right up there with having their kids go hang gliding or bungee jumping.

I would be damned before I would let anyone—let alone parents who are supposed to know better—win a game that way.

"If you want to call the game, it's fine with me," I said, trying not to sound as angry as I felt. "I'm happy to end it right now. But you realize, of course, that if we do, the runs you scored in the top of the inning won't count."

"Why?" three of the mothers asked at once.

"Because we haven't had a chance to hit yet in the sixth inning. It wouldn't be fair to count the runs you scored in an inning where we weren't allowed to bat. We'd have to go back to the last *full* inning to figure out how the game should end.

"If you'll remember, at the end of the fifth we were ahead 25-24, and we can end the game there if you want. That'll be fine with me. I'm tired, hungry, and would love to have some dinner. Just let me go tell my kids that we won, and we can all pack up all our stuff and go home. Otherwise, why don't we give my kids a chance to hit, and we'll go ahead with the bottom of the sixth with us trailing by a run."

All of a sudden the mothers weren't so insistent that the game be stopped. In fact, now that I had explained that stopping the game would result in their team losing, they thought ending the game was a terrible idea. Fair play, they said, mandated that my team get a chance to hit.

"It really isn't all that dark," they said.

"It wouldn't be fair to your kids," they said.

"Why don't we keep playing," they said.

I couldn't believe it. Now they were willing to continue the game—*just so they wouldn't lose*. This was the win-at-all-cost attitude that I had been fearing all along—*but it was coming from the mothers*.

There was nothing to be gained by continuing the game— no official league standings would be affected, no potential batting titles were on the line, no most valuable player awards would be jeopardized. Our league didn't have any of those things. They wanted to keep playing, *just so they could leave and say that their kids had won*.

Jeez.

This was far from an isolated instance. It was always a mother on the opposing team who checked to see that everyone on my team—especially the weaker hitters—got a chance to bat. (Just as everyone had to play the field the entire game, everybody also had to hit.) It was the mothers who tracked, in remarkable detail, where their child hit in the batting order, and it was the mothers who screamed loudest at the umpires on any call that was remotely close.

Now that I think about it, it was always a mother who kept score and sometimes "miscounted," always, it seemed, in her team's favor.

This wasn't cute or endearing. It was rapidly becoming a pain in the neck.

Fortunately, in this particular case, it turned out all right.

We ended up scoring just 1 run in the bottom of the sixth and the game ended in a 26-26 tie. While we had the option of scheduling extra innings at some other time, both Dan and I were more than happy to leave it at that.

After the game, I went to Dan and a couple of other coaches who were finishing up their games and we all exchanged horror stories about mothers.

We tried to be understanding. Sure you can get caught up in the excitement of the game, we told each other. And maybe if you didn't play competitive sports as a kid—and all of the mothers were raised at a time when girls were barred from playing Little League baseball—you might be tempted to take the games too seriously. Still, we agreed, something had to be done.

The easy thing was to compile a list that showed when the sun would set each day. We did and, starting the following season, when you signed up to be a coach, in addition to getting bats, balls, and bases, you received a sheet of paper that listed the exact time the sun would set during all regularly scheduled games, and you were told that no matter what, no inning could start after sunset.

What was far harder was figuring out what should be done with the mothers. We went to Sherry Cavise who, as a mother of two Little Leaguers, had experienced the yelling firsthand. In fact, she had agreed to be league commissioner in the hope of ending some of the silliness that had surrounded the games in the past. Sherry said she could write a note to the parents reminding them that league play was supposed to be a learning experience. By screaming, yelling, and generally behaving far worse than any of the children, parents were putting far too much pressure on their kids in addition to setting a poor example. (I thought the note idea was fine, but I still wish my suggestion that all parents be required to wear a gag at future

81

games had been adopted. Nobody, I'm afraid, has taken me seriously.)

Sherry said she'd write the letter and we could hope for the best. Frankly, I had my doubts.

As we were walking off the field after the "twilight game," two of my parents commented to me that we were still undefeated. The people making the comment, were, of course, mothers.

12

I Never Knew the Trains Left the Station That Early

I'm going to get philosophical for a minute. Please bear with me. It won't take long.

I think there are three truly great lies of our time. Oh sure, there are a bunch of others such as "No new taxes"; or "This is a rebuilding year"; or the ever-popular "I'll never lie to you." But if people were like Pinocchio, the following three statements would cause their noses to grow at least a foot.

In no particular order, they are:

1. "True, we're both very busy but we spend quality time with the children."

2. "It was an amiable divorce."

3. "He's decided to go on the daddy track."

Let's take them one at a time.

"Quality time" is inherently silly. The concept—which in

a nutshell says it isn't how much time you spend with your kids, but what you do with them during that time—is goofy because the entire premise is built on something that isn't true.

The idea of quality time—which was created by overworked parents who were looking for a way to assuage their guilt—assumes that during the fifteen, twenty, or thirty minutes they have during a day to spend with their kids, the kids will want to spend those same fifteen, twenty, or thirty minutes with them.

How do you know?

How do you know ahead of time that your kids won't be off at a friend's house during those 900 to 1,800 seconds—or won't be hopelessly involved in a fourteenth rerun of a Teenage Mutant Ninja Turtles cartoon? And how do you know that your kid won't simply be in a bad mood during those designated minutes and would prefer to be left alone?

It's hard enough scheduling a tune-up on your car; how do you plan quality time in advance?

"Amiable divorce" is another idea that has never made sense to me. If you are so amiable, how come you're divorced?

The "daddy track" is no different.

The problem—which was discovered by women a long time ago—is that you just can't have it all. While everyone says it is a good idea for fathers to spend more time with their children—and then wistfully add how they wish their fathers had spent more time with them when they were growing up—nobody is willing to do anything about it.

"You've got two practices during the week—hey, that's really great, Paul. I sure did value those few times when my Dad and I would throw the old ball around. But, hey, this isn't going to affect that report/memo/letter/executive summary that is due tomorrow/next week/before the millennium, is it?"

"Got a coaches meeting tonight, huh? No problem. Just have that piece you're editing on my desk before I get in tomorrow" (which, of course, is exactly when it was due).

"Hey, you got into the playoffs? That's great. We have a staff meeting at five-thirty. Really need you there, big guy."

The message is quite clear. It's all very nice to volunteer to coach and spend more time with your kids—something that corporate America devotedly believes in because a happy employee is a productive employee—just don't let it interfere with your workload.

Now, even corporate America knows that attitude is a bit harsh in the kinder, gentler nineties, and so they created the "daddy track."

The phrase first started popping up in women's magazines in the early 1980s and spread to places like *Time* and *Newsweek* a couple of years later.

Fittingly enough, the term daddy track did not make it into the business press in any serious way until *Business Week* highlighted the concept on the cover in spring 1991. Even then it wasn't the cover story; it was merely listed on the cover as one of the stories that would receive a lot of space inside.

I say that it was fitting, because neither business readers— nor business leaders, or society in general, for that matter— has ever really been comfortable with the concept of a man putting his family before his career.

Oh, the daddy track is fine in theory of course, everyone agrees. Sort of a maternity leave/mommy track for guys, right? Good idea.

And therein lies the problem. It's only an idea and one that no one in business wishes you'd take them up on. That's a point they get across in any number of ways.

If you opt to reduce your workload in order to spend more time with your family people start calling you—jokingly, of course—"Mr. Mom" (from the movie starring Michael Keaton) to your face, and saying things like "I'm not really sure he is serious about his job" behind your back.

So while some of the largest companies have given men the option of reducing their workload (and paycheck) in order to spend more time with the kids, it's not particularly surprising that only a miniscule number of men have taken their companies up on the offer.

Now who knows? Maybe the refusal of guys—me among them, let me hasten to point out—to reduce their workload is silly macho posturing. It might well be possible to spend time, serious time, with the kids while reducing your workload a bit, and not hurt your career. It might even be possible for a guy to get off the fast track for a while to devote more time to his family, then hop back on when it's more convenient, although I've never known a guy who's done it. In fact, I know of very few women who have done it.

But whatever the reality, my choice was to keep working full-time at a job that requires some travel and bizarre hours upon occasion, and to still try to coach at two games and a practice each week. If that's the route you take, you find yourself in some intriguing dilemmas.

For starters, you learn how to change your clothes in some interesting places.

I've never understood why baseball managers wear uniforms. Basketball coaches don't. They show up to work in suits and ties. Football coaches don't. They wear sweaters when it's nice out, and parkas when the games are played during weather that is perfect for the aptly named Bears and Vikings. You never see them in shoulder pads as they pace the sidelines.

But baseball is different. If you manage or coach at the big league level you wear a uniform, usually with a beer belly spilling over your belt. And since we at Little League do everything possible to emulate the big boys, it means our managers wear uniforms, too. (Our bellies are smaller, but then again, we are usually younger.)

It's kind of cute actually. Except when you are rushing from work, dressed in a suit, tie, and dress shoes and you're trying to get to a game that's starting at five-thirty.

One alternative would be going to work with the uniform on, but it would make it tough to get a good table at a Manhattan restaurant for lunch. While some of the better places have eased their dress code a bit—maitre d's are no longer apoplectic if you show up to dine without wearing a tie—the idea of walking into someplace like Lutèce wearing a pale blue T-shirt that says "Holmdel Baseball" on it, with the letters H(olmdel) Y(outh) A(thletic) A(ssociation) in baseballs extending across your chest might prove to be too much for even the most relaxed maitre d'.

The obvious solution would be to get home early and change before the game. But when you live fifty miles from the office as I do, that's a lot easier than it sounds. There just isn't time to take a fifty-five-minute train ride, then drive from the train station to the house (five miles), change and then drive another three miles to the field, if you are planning to get anything done at work that day. To meet that kind of schedule would mean leaving work just before lunch, and even for a writer that would be an extremely early slide.

So, I learned to change clothes on the train. It was sort of like being Clark Kent, but instead of rushing into a phone booth and donning my Superman cape at supersonic speed, I walked into the restroom on the 3:42 out of Manhattan, a room that measures four by four, and tried to take off my suit and put on my Little League outfit (T-shirt, sweatpants, sneakers), while the train hit every rut on the North Jersey

Coast Line as it headed south toward Matawan, the station closest to my home.

There were other interesting changes in my daily routine as well. For one thing, all nonmandatory meetings were moved to days when we didn't have a practice or a game. And I also fiddled with my travel schedule. Instead of looking for airlines that awarded the most frequent-flyer miles, I now picked flights based solely on whether they could get me back in time for the first pitch.

And that could lead to some interesting situations. For example, *Inc.*'s tenth anniversary party was going to be held in Boston on a Friday night, the day before our fourth game of the season. A game that would begin at 9:00 A.M.

The party—a serious black-tie affair—was spectacular. Everyone who worked for the magazine, no matter where in the world they worked, was flown in and put up at one of Boston's fancier hotels. The party favors were a wine bucket and two champagne glasses from Tiffany's, and everyone received a leather-bound copy of the tenth anniversary issue, inscribed with a personal note from the magazine's founder and chairman, Bernie Goldhirsh.

The party itself was held on what can only be described as a mini luxury liner that cruised around Boston Harbor and then went out to sea, while waiters passed round hors d'oeuvres and champagne before the sit-down dinner. Little Anthony, yes, *that* Little Anthony ("Tears on My Pillow"; "Going Out of My Head") performed and was constantly interrupted by applause from the primarily thirty-something crowd, which remembered singing along with, or making out to, the songs that Little Anthony and the Imperials had made famous more than twenty years before. (The Imperials, alas, couldn't make it.)

It was great but by the time I got back to my hotel room it was 3:30 A.M. Nonetheless, feeling much the worse for wear—I had exceeded my two-drink limit by at least one—I was on the 6:30 A.M. Boston to Newark flight, dressed in full uniform. (Although there were times that, for whatever reason, I couldn't change on the train and ended up managing in suit pants, dress shoes, and my Little League T-shirt, I thought the idea of managing in black tie was a bit much. It was, however, tempting.)

But for all the logistical difficulties, coaching brought certain benefits to my everyday working life as well.

For one thing, it became a perfect excuse for not dealing with people—specifically PR people.

Public relations people are one of the banes of any reporter's existence. While they are paid quite handsomely to promote the best interests of their client, I've yet to meet more than a handful who understand the magazine they're pitching, or who will take no for an answer once it becomes clear that the story they're suggesting isn't appropriate.

After a while you can get tired of explaining for the sixth time to the same person that you work for a magazine that specializes in covering small companies, and no, you really don't think an interview with the executive senior vice-president of Intergalactic Oil, a *Fortune* 2 company, would be appropriate for our readers.

Little League gave me the perfect out.

Instead of making excuses or thinking of reasons not to meet people who wouldn't be right for the magazine, I started saying things like, "Gee, Mr. Intergalactic himself is going to be in town on Tuesday? Gosh, I'd love to spend some time with him and hear his latest thoughts on international energy exploration and worldwide conservation strategies, but we have a Little League game that day and, unfortunately, I'm going to be leaving early. You understand, don't you? Maybe we could do it another time."

Little League also served as the perfect excuse for getting off the phone. When someone—invariably another PR person—had gone on for too long, I simply said there was a call on the other line. The fictitious call was always from my assistant coach who wanted to talk about strategy, or the league president who wanted to move the starting time of a game. Sometimes it was from one of the kids on the team who wanted to know where he would be playing that night. (At one time or another I actually did get all those calls at work.) In any event, I had to get off the phone now. Sorry.

It worked wonders in my personal life, too. Those chatty folks up the street—the ones who could spend hours showing you the video they took of the birth of their second child (they had hired a film crew)—want to have us over for a barbeque on Saturday?

"Love to but you know, we have a Little League game that Saturday and who knows what kind of mood I'm going to be in after that. This is a pivotal game, you know, and I'd hate to think about what I'm going to be like if we lose. Maybe we can catch that video after the season is over."

All, in all, I'd have to say the pluses outweighed the minuses.

13

Game #4: When Rooting for the Yankees Was Like Rooting for U.S. Steel

Here's something I had worried about since our first practice: would the kids get better as the season progressed?

It wasn't an idle question.

Common sense dictates that if you do anything long enough you're bound to show improvement. Your first attempts at walking, riding a bike, and kissing are—as a rule—pretty comical, but with practice you get better.

I had thought the same would hold true for our team's ability to play baseball but I was beginning to have my doubts.

As we took the field for our fourth game we were entering the fourth week of the season, and there really hadn't been much, if any, improvement from our very first practice. Michael Goodman still flinched each time I pitched to him, Stevie's fielding, to be charitable, needed work (Olé! And another ball goes bouncing right by him), and Peter still tried to hog anything hit anywhere on the field.

The kids and I had talked about what they were supposed to do until I was just about out of breath, but still the team looked about as good as it did four weeks ago. Not very.

True, we still hadn't lost a game but that was because the competition was even worse than we were. Our lack of improvement was starting to worry me.

But all my troubles melted like lemon drops in game #4. It was just like a scene from *The Music Man*.

You remember the plot. Robert Preston plays con man Professor Harold Hill, whose latest scam is to convince the good citizens of River City, Iowa, that they need to start a marching band to keep their kids out of trouble after school. And, as it turns out, Hill just happens to be selling all the instruments they'll need to start that band.

Well, the town elders of River City agree to his sales pitch on one condition: the professor has to teach their kids how to play. Now Preston doesn't know the first thing about teaching music. (If you have already substituted "baseball" for "music" you understand why I identified with the story line.) So in the tradition of con men everywhere, he decides to fake it. His advice to the kids: If you *think* the "Minuet in G," you'll be able to play the "Minuet in G."

The kids practice and practice and practice *thinking* the "Minuet in G," but when it's time to actually *play* the "Minuet in G," all that comes out is a series of squeaks and squawks and god-awful noise.

However, on the day of the big recital, the deadline Preston has been given for teaching the kids to play, or face being jailed for being the con man he actually is, lo and behold, the kids actually play the "Minuet in G."

Sort of.

Well, I think of game #4 as our "Minuet in G." For the first time since the season began we played baseball.

Sort of.

Michael Goodman, as calm as you please, stood up at the plate, didn't flinch as the pitch came toward him, and stroked a clean single to right his first time up. (From the exchange of high fives all around, you would have thought he had won the seventh game of the World Series single-handedly.) Stevie actually stayed *directly* in front of a ground ball and caught it, and Peter, playing center field, decided to let the second baseman field a ground ball that was hit between first and second.

Watching all this, I was more than pleased. I was shocked. In a nutshell, my reaction (to mix musicals for a moment) was: "By Jove, I think they've got it."

For a couple of moments out there it actually looked like baseball.

Now nobody could start comparing us to the 1927 Yankees, at least not yet.

For one thing, there was no guarantee that the improvement was going to last. After hitting his single, Michael Goodman reverted to form on his next at-bat. On the very first pitch he flinched, even though the ball was nowhere near him.

For another, for all their improvement these were still little kids. An example: when the game bogged down in the fourth inning due to a long series of foul balls, John McCarthy simply walked away from his position in left field and began climbing a nearby jungle gym. After watching the opposing coach throw somewhere around twenty-five or thirty pitches to a kid, who either fouled them off or just refused to swing, I couldn't blame him.

Still, it was clear that we were getting better. One quick example will prove the point.

We finally mastered the ninth batter rule.

Ever since the season began, I had tried to explain what we should do when the ninth batter was up and a ball was hit to the outfield. If you'll remember, under the ninth batter rule the only way the inning could end, once a ball that had hit the ground reached the outfield, was for a fielder to step on home plate while holding the ball. Since that was the rule, it wasn't surprising that all the other coaches simply told the outfielder to pick up the ball and run it home.

True, as they were quick to concede, that advice wasn't calculated to cut down on scoring. (As the outfielder was running in, the batter and whoever was on base would be running as hard as they could, trying to get home.) But as they explained to their kids—and to me—having the outfielder run the ball home reduced the number of things that could go wrong.

If the outfielder actually threw the ball toward home plate, there was no guarantee that the ball would end up anywhere near there. It was not uncommon for the right fielder to pick up the ball and have his throw end up in center. It violated all known laws of physics, but it happened a lot. And even if he did manage to find home plate with his throw, the odds were low that there would be anyone there who could catch it. Because there were no passed balls, wild pitches, or stealing, teams tended to play their worst fielders at catcher since there really was no need for the catcher to catch anything. Given all this, it made sense to have the kids run the ball in to home plate.

I understood the thinking—heck, deep down I agreed with it—but having a kid run in from right field to make a play at home plate just didn't strike me as baseball.

What I wanted to see happen was this: once the baseball was hit into the outfield, the first baseman would rush in to cover home. (We almost never played with a catcher.) The outfielder would pick up the ball and throw it to the waiting first baseman, who would catch it and step on the plate. The side would be retired and I'd look like a genius.

If it worked.

It sounded fine in theory. However, reality turned out to be quite different.

For one thing, the first baseman—and it really didn't matter who we put there—usually forgot what he was supposed to do. He would stand at first and watch as the outfielder picked up the ball and threw it toward a totally unoccupied home plate. The ball would just roll and roll, while the batter—and whoever was on the bases—came around to score.

Sometimes the first baseman would remember he was supposed to cover home but he would leave too early. Remember, one way the inning could end, even with the ninth batter at the plate, was on a routine out. Someone could catch a fly ball, or an infielder could pick up a ground ball and throw to first.

At least he could if the first baseman was there. On more than one occasion, the first baseman broke for home as soon as the ball was hit, never looking to see that the ball was still in the infield. Whoever fielded the grounder would look toward first, see that nobody was there, and then freeze. (Unfortunately, the batter, and the runners on base, didn't.)

Through the first three games, my plan for handling the ninth batter rule hadn't worked very well. In fact, it hadn't worked at all. So much for being a genius.

However, I looked a whole lot smarter in game #4. With runners on first and second in the first, the ninth batter hit a single to center, where Wei Yang was playing. He fielded it cleanly and threw the ball perfectly to Agam at shortstop.

While this was going on Michael Roman, who was playing

95

first base, watched to make sure that the ball would reach the outfield. (There had been a chance that Takeshi, who was playing right on second base, might have made the play, but the ball was just beyond his reach.) Once Michael saw the ball go through, he broke toward home plate and was waiting there for Agam's perfect one-bounce relay. The ball got there before the runner from second did and no runs scored.

After a play like that, there was no way we could lose— and we didn't.

This was the first game where we caught more balls than we missed and also the first game in which everyone got a hit, although the official scorer (me) was fairly liberal. If you got on base for anything other than hitting into a force play, you were credited with a hit. Someone dropped your pop-up? Hit. A ground ball went through a fielder's legs? Hit. You get the idea. With those as the parameters, it was hard to find someone on our team who was hitting less than .500.

We had some legitimate shots, though. Michael Roman finally lived up to his preseason promise by hitting two real home runs, and Justin Marconi, now fully accustomed to the Justin Marconi Rule of Pitching, hit a clean double in each of his three trips to the plate.

Good defense and good hitting almost always guarantee an easy win. It did here.

There's a great line attributable to one of the early owners of the N.Y. Yankees, a man who was running the club while George Steinbrenner was still a toddler in Cleveland. When asked to describe the perfect ball game he said: "We score nine runs in the first and slowly pull away."

We came close. We scored 6 in the first, 5 in the second, and another 6 in the third. Final score: 28-9.

We're now 3-0-1. Gosh, this is getting to be fun.

14

The Cheatin' Coach
and Other Tales

Four games into the season I knew that coaches came in three varieties—and I wasn't particularly fond of two of the flavors.

First were the coaches like Tim, who acted more as a baby-sitter than a coach. Oh, they'd give an occasional bit of instruction ("Jeffrey, try to keep your eyes open when you swing") but only a bit. They basically saw their job as making sure that the kids didn't kill themselves during practices or games. That point should not be glossed over too quickly. When you allow six-, seven-, and eight-year-olds to wander around carrying 25-ounce pieces of wood (bats), chaos—and cracked skulls—can result. Each coach was required to pass a Red Cross–approved first-aid course before he was given his whistle.

The problem with coaches like Tim was that they didn't

want the games to be competitive at all and they'd invariably fold, rather than argue, on any close play.

But while their intentions were good—nobody wants Little League games to be decided by which coach can scream the loudest—their approach just wasn't fair to the kids they were coaching.

While the kids didn't consider the games to be a matter of life and death, they took the game seriously, while it was going on. But once it was over, it was over. To them Little League was nothing more than recess with uniforms; win or lose they would see their friends on the other team at school the next day. However, nobody wanted to go home with an 0-10 record at the end of the season. If you were concerned about making sure that the kids had fun, it seemed to me that you had to try to win at least a few games. Losing all the time is no fun, no matter how old you are.

And if a coach was going to win at least a couple of games, he had to offer more than full-time baby-sitting with a dash of instruction thrown in. He had to make sure that the kids on his team actually got better as the season progressed. Part of your responsibility as a coach, it seemed to me, was explaining to the kids what they were doing right—and wrong—and suggesting ways they could improve.

After all, the kids on my team were (finally) getting better, as our experience in game #4 ("Minuet in G") showed, and a quick look around the league showed that most of the other teams were improving as well.

True, neither they, nor us, were ready to take on the New York Mets—heck, we probably would have been killed if we'd played against a team made up of third and fourth graders—but the fact was we *were* getting better, and the kids liked that. It's more fun to play baseball if you hit the ball more times than you miss it, and you know that you are

98

catching balls today that you would have dropped yesterday. As long as you're improving, you can dream of being the next Ken Griffey, Jr., or of striking out Wade Boggs with the bases loaded in the seventh game of the World Series.

The Tims of the world never understood that. They equated winning with screaming and yelling over every call that didn't go their way, and since they didn't want to yell, they just let everyone else get *their* way.

Probably worse, at least from my perspective, was that Tim and the other coach who shared his "laid-back" approach to managing, never really seemed to be having fun out on the field.

Starting when I was fifteen and continuing through my senior year in college, I worked as a camp counselor each summer and had an absolutely wonderful time. Kids are fun. They are constantly upbeat, passionate about everything— they either absolutely love something ("killer" dodge ball) or hate it (swimming lessons)—and are always in motion.

I am not a childhood idolizer. I don't think kids are always the most wonderful things on the planet. They can be vicious, especially to other kids who are different (fat, not particularly bright, or nonathletic). And they are often lacking in sense— common or otherwise. (Why, as a childhood rite seems to demand, would anyone think it was a good idea to throw a large firecracker into a metal garbage can, screw the lid on tight, and then stand six inches away to see what happens?)

But for the most part, kids are a lot more fun to be around than most grown-ups I know. Part of the reason for that is their complete commitment to whatever they are doing. Whether they are trying to catch worms or throwing sticks across a river, kids give the activity their total concentration.

That is certainly true when they play baseball, and for me part of the fun of coaching was sharing their excitement.

Between the games, practices, coaches meetings, and the like, Little League was taking more than fifteen hours a week. Why would anyone agree to commit that amount of time and try—as Tim seemed to be doing—to remain detached? No one said you had to be a jerk and treat each game as if your entire professional career depended on it. Being at least twenty-five years older than the kids, you ought to have *some* perspective about all this. But if coaching wasn't fun, why were you doing it?

Tim never seemed to be having much fun. And his kids weren't getting better, and both of those things were a shame.

Tim never seemed to smile during the games, never held an extra practice to work on areas where his kids needed help—their fielding was particularly atrocious—in addition to refusing to be competitive. He never stuck up for his kids, even when it was clear that they had beaten out an infield hit or caught a ball that had been ruled a trap.

In the only game Tim didn't lose he played the one other coach who shared his noncompetitive-at-all-costs-I-am-going-to-be-detached-no-matter-what attitude. Fittingly enough, that game ended in a tie.

The bulk of the other managers—six, including me—fell into the middle category of the coaching ranks. We were all there because we'd had killer coaches when we played Little League and would be damned if we let some out-of-shape bully yell at our kids, and/or we wanted to teach the kids a little bit of baseball strategy as well. For example, I told all the kids that if they were ever confused about where to throw the ball, look where the runner is and throw to the base ahead. That meant if the batter hit a single and you picked up the ball in the outfield, your throw should be to second base. A double? The play would be to third, and so on. Just knowing that much would put them ahead of some major league players.

Baseball was our favorite sport and the six of us also had something else in common. We wanted to win—not at all costs, mind you—but we wanted to win. Actually, to be perfectly accurate, we didn't want to lose. It turned out that all of us shared the fear of going 0-for-the-season. Fortunately for us, as long as Tim and his friend were around we probably would finish no worse than ninth, since we were bound to beat their two teams.

When the six of us played each other, things went reasonably well. We each bent over backward to make sure we didn't make calls that favored only our teams; nobody had a problem with giving particularly bad hitters four strikes and occasionally five. (When *our* kids complained, we simply said that the batter's two-strike swing, where he missed the ball by at least three feet, had resulted in a foul ball.) And once everybody had won at least one game, we could even deal with each other as friendly adversaries. We traded horror stories about the mothers ("You mean she really called you at eleven-thirty at night to complain where you were batting her kid in the lineup?"), slandered the various people running for the Board of Education, and generally had a good time.

Dealing with the remaining three coaches was anything but fun.

They were out to win. Period. And they saw absolutely nothing funny about it.

Of the three Alex was almost tolerable. He didn't cheat. He just did absolutely everything by the book, if there was a book to follow. If there wasn't, he'd go to extremes to give his team an edge.

An example. There is a rule, which apparently has existed

101

for as long as the Holmdel Youth Athletic Association (HYAA) has been around, that says all kids playing Little League must wear white pants during every game. It's an absolutely stupid rule. The very last color you want Peter and his friends to wear when they are outside is white. There seems to be a genetic disposition in boys to dive into dirt whenever they see it. That trait instantly surfaces any time a boy steps on a baseball field.

The combination of all that nice, even dirt—the fields are raked before every game—coupled with a sudden overwhelming desire to emulate their favorite big league ballplayer, can only result in disaster if you require the kids to wear white anywhere on their bodies. By the time they get done making diving catches, headfirst slides into second base, and falling to the ground to avoid pitches that are nowhere near them, those white pants are going to be filthy long before it's time to go home.

Apparently there had been talk years before of changing to a more reasonable color—gray or black leap to mind—but for whatever reason, it had never happened. By the time I became manager, white had become a "tradition" and I was told, in no uncertain terms, that we weren't about to tamper with tradition.

So, white pants it would be, and that's what I told all the kids to wear. But when you are seven or eight, you tend to forget things. Or it takes your mother a bit longer than expected to get those white pants clean or . . .

Whatever the reason, my kids would occasionally forget to show up wearing either their blue T-shirts or—horrors!—their white pants.

I didn't much care. But Alex did. When two of my kids—and Peter was one of them—showed up for a game against

Alex's team wearing pants that weren't white, Alex made a big point of delaying the first pitch.

He pointed to Peter and the other offender, Michael Roman, and said: "They're not wearing white."

"Yeah, I guess they forgot," I said.

"You know, I could make you forfeit the game."

"Really?"

"Yes," Alex said. "It's in the rules. I can show you if you want." And with that he started walking back toward the dugout, presumably to get the twenty-five pages of mimeographed rules we had been handed before the season began.

"Hey, Alex. That's okay. I believe you. But if we don't have any standings and the games don't really count, what's the purpose of making someone forfeit?"

"The kids have to know there are rules in this world, that's why. The rules say they are supposed to wear white pants, so they're supposed to wear white pants."

I couldn't argue with that. Since I didn't understand how anyone could think this way, I couldn't very well argue with it.

I promised Alex that I would try to have my kids behave better in the future.

The real purpose of Alex's complaining was to let me know I owed him one. Since he didn't demand that I forfeit—and indeed he could have; when I went home I looked up the rule—he expected to get the benefit of the doubt on the first close play.

And so, like I jerk, I gave it him. And once I did, he didn't let up. He tracked the number of times I called close plays against him, always making sure I knew when more calls had been called my way than his. He took notes to see that all my kids batted in order, double-checked to see that everyone touched all the bases when a home run was hit, and generally acted like an anal-retentive jerk. If there was a rule, Alex made sure it was enforced.

If there wasn't a rule, you could be sure Alex would do whatever it would take to win. Take the matter of practices. It was *suggested* teams hold one practice a week. Suggested, but not mandated. Since it was hard enough for some of the coaches and kids to make two games a week, *requiring* a practice was a bit much. So the practice was optional, and holding it once a week was only a suggestion.

There was no rule saying you had to have a practice and that, as Alex was quick to understand, meant that there wasn't a *rule* saying you couldn't have more than one.

Since there wasn't a rule, Alex decided that he would hold practice *every single day*. If there wasn't a game, you knew his kids would be out there working on hitting the cutoff man, practicing double plays (Double plays! My kids had enough trouble catching the ball, let alone going for two), and working on their hitting. Every day, Sundays included, for at least an hour.

Having a practice every day was typical of something Alex would do. He was annoying, to say the least.

Scott and Sam, however, were obnoxious.

To be blunt, they cheated. Constantly.

Even more bothersome, they weren't good at it.

For all intents and purposes Scott and Sam were interchangeable. The only difference was that Scott understood how baseball was played and Sam didn't. As a result, Scott's cheating allowed him to win, Sam's didn't—which only served to make him more obnoxious.

Sam, who owned an optical supply business, reminded me of several trial lawyers I knew. All lawyers are egotistical, but the people who appear in court take ego to the limits of human endurance. In their eyes, it's them against the world and they figure that makes the odds just about even.

One of the images that I will remember to my dying day is watching the aptly named defense attorney Michael Tigar strutting into the courtroom during the Abscam trials. Tigar flung open the swinging gate that separated the spectator seating area from the attorney tables as if he were entering a 1880s saloon ready for a gunfight. Not surprisingly, if you looked down, you saw Tigar was wearing cowboy boots.

Now the best attorneys keep their combativeness under control, using their theatrics only when it will do the most good. Those who aren't as good consistently badger every witness and contest every point—even the ones that are clearly hopeless or unimportant—and generally make a pain out of themselves.

Whatever edge they gain by catching people in insignificant mistakes, they more than lose by alienating the judge and jury. ("You told the jury you've been a police officer for nineteen years," said one defense attorney I covered, long before I became a business writer, who was trying to attack the credibility of the cop who had been the first to arrive at an accident. "But the truth is, you've barely been on the force eighteen years, isn't it. *Isn't it!*" His client was convicted.)

Like a bad lawyer, Sam alienated everyone he came in contact with.

A reasonably close play at first, where his runner was out by a step? Sam would yell, "Safe!"

Somebody on his team hit a ball that was foul by six inches? He'd tell you it was fair all the way.

His kid swung and came nowhere close to hitting the ball? Sam would rule he foul-tipped it and give the kid another swing.

By the end of the second game his reputation had gotten around the league. As a result, not only was he *not* getting the benefit of the doubt, it was more than likely that he was losing more than his fair share of the close calls.

Here's why. When I knew I'd be playing Sam's team, I did what every other coach in the league had learned to do. I arranged to have two parents—one from my team and one from Sam's—do the umpiring. "That way we can concentrate on helping the kids," all the coaches told Sam. And the parents, even the ones on his team, quickly became fed up with Sam's rantings and ravings over every call. It got so bad that the parents of the kids *on his own team* seemed to go out of their way to make rulings against him, because he was so obnoxious.

If you're not going to get half the breaks you are at a disadvantage, and Sam compounded his problem by not understanding the game or the ability of his players.

Fascinated by the pro game, Sam would instruct his kids to play baseball as the big leaguers do: go for double plays, try to make the diving catch, and always be aggressive on the base paths.

That strategy might have worked if Sam had been managing a pro team. But he wasn't. When you have a kid playing first base who has enough problems trying to catch a ball and remembering to step on the base, the idea of having him do anything complicated—like throwing to the shortstop covering second, and then rushing back to first to try to complete a 3-6-3 double play—is not going to rank among the best ideas the world has ever known.

But Sam kept on telling his kids to try to make the double play, and he also kept telling them to try to stretch singles into doubles. And his kids—through absolutely no fault of their own—kept letting him down. Double play balls would be dropped at second base, and his runners kept getting thrown out trying to take the extra base.

After a couple of games of watching this happen time after time, you would have thought Sam would have learned his lesson.

You would have thought wrong.

Like a bad gambler on a losing streak, the more times Sam's "system" failed, the more convinced he was that his luck would soon turn. He would have his kids take more and more risks in anticipation of the moment when the breaks would finally go his way. They never did.

Part of the reason for that was that Sam was a truly lousy judge of talent, especially when it came to evaluating his son.

Sammy was just not that good but to hear Sam tell it, Jose Canseco was supposed to start looking over his shoulder. If Jose had ever seen Sammy play, he would have known that his $5 million a year salary was safe.

Sam would put his son at shortstop and disaster would soon follow. It wasn't that Sammy was awful. He wasn't. It was just that he wasn't a pressure ballplayer. He'd consistently make the easy play and even the more difficult ones in the early innings, and even in the later ones, as long as the score was lopsided one way or the other. However, once the game was on the line, Sammy would tense up and make a bad throw or let the ball squirt between his legs. His father would make excuses ("It took a bad hop"; "The first baseman should have caught the throw" that sailed five feet over his head) and Sam's team would lose another one.

If you manage badly and ask your kids to do too much, even heavy-handed cheating won't help. At the end of the first four games, Sam's team was 0-4. They proceeded to lose every game—to hear Sam tell it they were robbed in every one—and even finished behind Tim's team.

So serious cheating didn't work.

However, the subtle kind—as employed by Scott—did pay off, and quite handsomely.

I knew I'd be having problems with Scott right away. A home builder who had made several million dollars during the real estate boom of the 1980s, Scott had recently sold his company and now dabbled as a venture capitalist. He'd put his money in various deals—he was partial to health clubs and new restaurants. If he did well his family could continue to live in what can only be described as Tara, across the highway from me. If he didn't—and you have to work really hard to blow $3 million of your own money—the unthinkable might happen. Scott might have to go back to work.

Now, real estate developers are, as a rule, not the most likable of folks. They are sort of like salesmen on steroids. They are utterly focused on the next deal. But the drive that makes them successful in business—and for all the justifiable criticism they receive, no one is going to argue that developers are not in one of the world's most competitive fields—can make them obnoxious in a supposedly friendly setting like Little League. And that was apparent at the first coaches' meeting. Scott asked that his team be given black shirts.

When the season starts each team is assigned a color. Not surprisingly, red is the most popular, and usually what happens is that whoever remembers to ask the league president for a specific color gets it. But nobody in the history of HYAA had ever asked for black. You play your games in the late spring and into the summer and it can get incredibly hot out there on the Little League field at noon on a Saturday. The last thing you want to do is wear a black shirt that absorbs the heat.

So why did Scott want black? "It's a scary color. People in

black are intimidating. It makes the kids look more impressive, more professional."

And Scott took that one step further. Before handing out the black shirts to his team, he had each kid's name—their last name—printed in large white letters on the back. (He was not alone in this. Tom Wilson, another coach, always put the kids' names on their shirts.) So had Scott stopped there nobody would have thought too much about it. But he didn't. He cheated—subtly—but he cheated nonetheless.

To Scott's credit, he was very clever about it. He only cheated when it was absolutely necessary, and then he did it in such a way that you weren't supposed to get mad at him. One example will suffice.

Scott always scouted the team he was going to play. Since everybody played on different days, it wasn't that hard to do. Obsessive? Yes. Hard? No. And since he really didn't have to worry about making a living, he had the time to do it.

So Scott would go to all the games and watch to see who your best players were, then act accordingly.

For example, when it came time to play us, Scott knew that Michael Goodman was absolutely no threat to hit anything. So, he didn't even wait for me to suggest that Michael get a fourth swing after he had missed the first three balls by a wide margin. Scott suggested it—at the top of his lungs, waving his arms so that everybody would see what a good guy he was. There was no danger that it was going to cost him anything. You could be certain that Michael would miss the next pitch as well. This way Scott could look like a hero at absolutely no cost—to him. There was, however, a cost to his opponent.

The idea behind Scott's "altruism" was simple. He was laying the groundwork for the cheating he'd do later.

If there was a close call in the late innings, you knew that

Scott was going to rule in favor of his team, no matter what the real call should have been. But since he had made such a show about bending over backward for the Michael Goodmans of the world, it was hard for anyone to get overly upset. Hey, would that nice coach, who was so kind to Michael Goodman, really decide to cheat us now?

Of course he would. That's why he was so nice in the first place.

This was all so unnecessary and bush. But I knew I would have to deal with it down the line. After the fourth game, Scott and I were managing the only two undefeated teams and we were scheduled to meet during the last game of the season.

15

Game #5: We Lose.
Yeaaah!

Starting with the third game, I lived with a constant and ever-increasing pressure: we were undefeated and I felt compelled to keep it that way.

It was a strange feeling—and like most of my reactions to my first year as a Little League manager, it was totally irrational.

Remember, I had begun my managerial career worrying that we wouldn't win a game. This was my first attempt at being the head coach of *anything* and I was petrified that a. I would let Peter down (at this age, he still thought I could lick most of the world's—well, at least most of his—problems single-handedly) and b. I was equally concerned that I would embarrass myself in front of everyone in town.

Those were my major worries going into the season but they had all disappeared after game one, when we won going away.

The second game was probably the best, from the point of view of my emotional well-being. There was no pressure at all. The worst that could happen was that we'd lose and our record would fall to 1-1. I could live with that. In fact, figuring the first game was just a fluke, I just assumed we'd lose game #2. So even though we were ahead the entire game, I kept waiting for something to go wrong. But it never did.

But it was right after the last pitch of the second game that I started to become concerned. Ridiculous, right? Ever since I found out I'd be coaching, I worried that we would never win a game, and the second that fear was put to rest forever, I found something else to worry about. How nuts is that? Instead of being happy, I began worrying that I would do something stupid in the next game that would jeopardize our (admittedly very modest) winning streak. I'd fail to realize who was a hot hitter and bury him down in the batting order, or I wouldn't notice that somebody wasn't as good a fielder as I'd first thought and he'd make an error at a pivotal moment and cost us the game. Increasingly, I felt it was all up to me to make sure that we kept winning.

The feeling didn't go away when we tied game #3, the infamous twilight game. Instead of taking the pressure off because we didn't win, I looked at the final score differently. Since we had tied the game that meant we *still* hadn't lost. We play only ten games, so the tie meant we had gone 30 percent of the season without a loss. My bizarre arithmetic just added to the pressure.

And that pressure got severe after game #4 (the "Minuet in G" game) where we won again. The only thing that made it slightly more tolerable was that the kids had played their best game of the year.

I couldn't tell anybody about how I was feeling. If I had, they'd have just confirmed the obvious. I was certifiable.

I could imagine the dialogue.

Me: "You know, I really feel under all this pressure all the time. We haven't lost yet and I know it's nuts but it's constantly on my mind."

Chorus, made up of three rational coaches: "You're feeling bad because your team hasn't lost yet? We still haven't won. How do you suppose that makes us feel?"

So, yes, I knew I was supposed to be counting my blessings before we played game #5 against a team that was 2-2 and was rumored to be lucky to have won both the games they did. But to be honest, I was hoping—just as I did before game #4—that we would lose.

And that's exactly what we did.

I didn't have to worry about making out a bad lineup or making the wrong decision when I told Michael Roman to try to score from second on a single. The kids managed to lose the game all by themselves—and in spectacular fashion.

In a word, they were awful.

I don't know if they were overconfident because they were undefeated through four games and had played spectacularly well two days before, or if I had been suffering from delusions about how good they really were, but they just couldn't do anything right today. You saw that in the very first inning.

We were the home team, which meant we were out in the field as the game began, and we were set in our usual defensive alignment with our best fielders up the middle. Peter played short, Takeshi second, and Agam was in center field. Given a choice, I'd want the ball hit to any of the three of them. If you hit the ball to Justin, or Michael Goodman, there was no telling what would happen. But if you hit it up the middle, we had a better than even chance of getting an out.

Well, Bill's team was accommodating. Their first batter hit

a soft line drive to center field. It was such a routine ball, I didn't even bother to yell out Agam's name.

The kids are supposed to call for the ball if they think they can make the catch but they never do, so invariably two things happen when someone hits the ball in the air. Either four kids run toward the ball at full speed and slam into each other while they are looking up trying to figure out where the ball will land, or four kids end up surrounding the ball and alternate between watching each other and the ball. It doesn't matter which scenario you choose. The result is the same either way: the ball hits the ground.

Since the kids never called for the ball, I started doing it for them. Any time a pop fly went up near third base, for example, I'd yell "Wei!" at the top of my lungs. That was my subtle signal that Wei should try to make the catch and everyone else should get out of his way.

On this one, though, there was no need to yell. First of all, the ball was hit directly at Agam. Second, it wasn't high enough off the ground for anyone else to even think about heading over and getting in his way. And third, and most important, there was no way Agam could miss it. The ball was the living definition of a "soft line drive." It was coming at Agam with all the speed of a softball thrown underhand by a five-year-old.

Agam took two steps in and then watched as the ball went floating right by him at waist level less than two feet away. By the time he had finally tracked it down—even soft line drives will roll for a while—the batter had scored. One pitch and we're down 1-0.

Before I even had a chance to say, "Hey guys, no big deal, let's settle down," the second batter was up and hit a nice, slow two-hopper to Peter. He fielded it cleanly, and I started to feel better. We had been down by a run before and Peter

114

fielding the grounder had to be an omen of good things to come. Just as I convinced myself everything was going to be fine, Peter promptly made one of the worst throws in the history of baseball over to first base. Don Mattingly, on his best day, couldn't have caught it. The ball was fifteen feet to the outfield side of first base and about twelve feet off the ground. Bobby Foley didn't even try to catch it. One base on the overthrow. So after two pitches we were down a run, there was a man on second, and nobody out.

It had to get better, right? Not necessarily. Two pitches later their third-place batter hit a solid ground ball at Takeshi.

Now Takeshi's entire game was built around consistency. Bobby Foley, Michael Roman, and Agam could hit the ball a lot farther and Peter was a flashier fielder, but on an everyday basis there was no one you could count on more than Takeshi.

When he was up at the plate, sure, he was going to swing from the heels on the first pitch but he always missed. And his second swing invariably produced a solid line drive up the middle. In the field, he could serve as a textbook guide for how to play second base. He would get his body directly in front of the ball—as he did here—bend his knees, lower his glove to where it was resting on the ground, and in this case watched as the ball promptly squirted between his legs and rolled agonizingly slowly into right field.

Here Bill's team had hit the ball three times in a row to our three best fielders, and instead of racing in from the field to get our turn at bat, we were now down 2-0, there was a man at first, and still nobody was out. Would this inning ever end?

It did, six batters later. Even then, we blew our play for the ninth batter rule when Bobby Foley forgot to cover home.

The only out we got in the inning occurred, ironically, when one of Bill's best batters struck out. As we came up to bat in the bottom of the first, we trailed 8-0.

Now you might think I was secretly pleased with the lop-sided score. After all, I had gone into the game hoping we'd lose and it was pretty clear that given the way we were playing, I was about to get my wish.

But instead of being happy as we came to bat, I did my best to rally the troops. If they could score 8 runs, we could score 9, I said. I wanted to win, even though that would just have increased the pressure heading into the next game. Why was I trying to organize a comeback, even though a victory would make me feel worse? I have absolutely no idea. (I *knew* I should have paid more attention to all those psychology courses back in school.)

But even though I didn't understand my motivation, I did know, as Peter went up to bat for us in the bottom of the first, that I really did want us to win. And I thought we could as I walked out to the mound to pitch. But as soon as I saw Peter step into the batter's box, I knew we were doomed. The Mel Hall stance had returned. There was Peter, waiting patiently at the plate, holding his bat high above his head.

"Peter," I said with all the exasperation that comes from being down 8-0 in the bottom of the first fully present in my voice.

"But, Dad, I really want to try it this way."

"No."

"Come on. Please?

"*No.*"

We had reached an impasse. Peter was standing at the plate, bat held high behind his head. I was standing on the mound, refusing to pitch. Everyone was watching and waiting.

While the parents sitting on lawn chairs beyond the foul

116

line were sympathetic—since they all were the proud owners of six-, seven-, or eight-year-olds they had gone through similar scenes many times themselves—sympathy will only take you so far. They wanted to get on with the game.

I did the only rational, mature thing possible. I systematically set off to strike out my son.

As you remember, the problem with batting like Mel Hall is that it is virtually impossible to hit anything that's thrown inside, especially if it's high and inside, and that's exactly where I threw the first pitch.

Peter swung and missed.

I put the second pitch in exactly same spot with exactly the same result.

Peter now had two strikes.

"Dad!"

"If you want to hit that way, it's fine with me," I said. "But I'm going to continue pitching you this way." I told you I was mature.

Now, there is a very good chance that *deliberately* striking out your son in a Little League game that is played in front of his friends can produce all kinds of emotional traumas. For one thing, it probably guarantees that he'll grow up being a hopeless devotee of John Bradshaw, the self-help author who believes that virtually everyone's problems stem from growing up in a dysfunctional family, but I didn't care. I was angry that we were behind 8-0. I was angry that I *cared* that we were behind 8-0, and I was angry that I had been walking around all week *worrying* about being *undefeated* to begin with. If Peter was determined to hit this way, I was determined to strike him out. Yep, there is no doubt about it. I can fall to the level of a seven-year-old with the best of them.

Would I have deliberately struck out Peter? We'll never know. Peter lowered his bat. Not to its normal position, but

117

enough so that he could get around on an inside pitch. I threw him another one inside, and he hit it hard but straight up. It came down in the glove of the shortstop. One out.

Takeshi was next and as always he swung as hard as he could at the first pitch. But this time—for the first time all season—he actually hit the ball, and he promptly discovered that there was another problem with swinging for the fences. Even if he did hit the ball with his killer swing, it wasn't going to go very far. Remember, Takeshi was the smallest kid on our team and used the lightest bat imaginable. So even his hardest swing was unlikely to produce a booming hit and this one didn't. Takeshi hit a routine fly ball to center field, identical in fact to the one that Agam had missed. *Their* center fielder caught it. Two up, two down.

Now this had never happened before. Peter almost always got on base, and Takeshi *always* did. Before that last swing, he had been batting 1.000. True, they had all been singles to center but neither rain, nor snow, nor gloom of night had kept Takeshi Fujiwara from hitting his single up the middle. With Peter and Takeshi getting on to lead off the game, invariably we would jump out to an early lead.

But here, when we needed the runs the most, Agam was coming up with nobody on. Seeing nobody on the base paths must have depressed him because he grounded out weakly. At the end of one we trailed 8-0.

It got marginally better from there, but only marginally. The kids managed to catch a couple of balls and Bobby Foley and Michael Roman managed to hit back-to-back home runs twice during the game, but we were never really in it. Final score: Bad Guys 14, Good Guys 9. We had lost our first game.

My feeling after the game gave new meaning to the word ambivalent. I didn't like losing, but on the other hand, our

118

winning streak was finally over and maybe I could get rid of the knot thatj had been in my stomach since the second week of the season.

At the halfway point, we were 3-1-1, and I was definitely ready for the All-Star break.

16

Reflections at the Halfway Mark

All-Star games, as a rule, are pretty boring. In pro football, the game is held after the Super Bowl and nobody—not even the most rabid fan, the kind of person who actually watches ESPN's gavel-to-gavel coverage of the NFL draft—cares about football once the Super Bowl is over.

Even the players don't care, something that the National Football League finally figured out. Tired of all the no-shows among both players and viewers, the NFL now schedules the game in Hawaii every February, figuring that's the only way they can get anyone to show up.

There are rumors that the National Hockey League plays an All-Star game each year, but frankly I don't believe it. Do you know anyone who lives south of the Canadian border who has actually seen an NHL All-Star game?

The NBA All-Star game *is* interesting because basketball is the only sport where players can show off on a one-on-one basis. And it's fun watching players like Isaiah Thomas of Detroit and Boston's Larry Bird playing on the same team and doing blind behind-the-back passes and 360-degree dunks to the cheers of a crammed auditorium.

But the NBA has gotten carried away with its own success. The game is now part of "an All-Star weekend," and by the time you've suffered through the slam-dunk contest, the 3-point shooting competition, the old-timers game, the old-timers slam-dunk contest and the like, you're too tired to care about the All-Star game itself.

Baseball's approach to showing off its best players isn't much better. For one thing, there are too many constraints on the game, designed, I suppose, to make sure no one gets hurt. The pitchers only go three innings, for example, and the players don't really care about the final score. Seeing somebody slide hard into second to break up a double play occurs about as often as finding a magazine that doesn't have Madonna on the cover.

I guess I always knew that baseball players basically saw the All-Star break as a three-day paid vacation, but I never wanted to admit it when I was growing up. When you're eight, you think everybody treats every game as a matter of life and death. After all, *you* do.

But whatever delusions I had were shattered by my boyhood idol, Mickey Charles Mantle. Listen as Mantle talks about All-Star games in *My Favorite Summer, 1956*:

> One thing I have always regretted . . . is that I never took the All-Star game seriously enough. I usually looked at it as a few days off to . . . rest and party. I liked to get

together with other guys in baseball that I didn't normally see, like Don Drysdale, Eddie Mathews, and Harvey Kuenn and hoist a few.

In 1967, the All-Star game was played in Anaheim . . . and I really didn't want to go. But they put me on the team anyway, and I had no choice.

I was [home] in Dallas the morning of the game, playing golf at the Preston Trails Country Club . . . and it was arranged for me to fly to the game. So I left the golf course and flew to Los Angeles. In Los Angeles, they picked me up in a helicopter and flew me to Anaheim, where I had a police escort to the ballpark. I got to the park just as the game was starting. I didn't even make the team picture.

I get . . . into uniform and walk into the dugout and I say to the players, "Hi, guys, how you doing." Hank [Bauer, who was managing the American League team] comes over and says, "You want to hit?"

"Sure," I said.

"O.K.," Hank said, "You hit for [American League pitcher Dean] Chance in the third inning . . . So I put on a helmet, and went up to hit against Juan Marichal and I struck out. I said good-bye to everybody and went back to the clubhouse, took off my uniform, got into my clothes, took the police car back to Anaheim airport, got in a helicopter and flew to Los Angeles and took a plane back to Dallas. The game went 15 innings, and by the time I got back to Preston Trails, [it] was still on. As I was sitting in the clubhouse watching the end of the game, some of the guys who saw me there said, "Damn, didn't we just see you strike out?"

So much for life and death.

But even if the players don't take the game seriously—and given the recent results, there's no indication that things have changed very much since Mantle's time—baseball's annual

122

midseason, three-day All-Star break serves a useful purpose. It gives owners, managers, players, and fans some time to reflect on how the season has been going. (It's also the time when your local sports section issues a report card on everyone on your team's roster.) And in Little League, just as in the big leagues, it also gives you a chance to think about what you want to do differently during the second half of the year.

At the first- and second-grade level, there is no All-Star game. It's hard to call somebody an All-Star—even if he's your best player—if he can only catch seven out of ten balls thrown to him. So our version of the All-Star break occurred during the Memorial Day weekend when the kids were off from school. Normally we have a game every Saturday, but during that weekend everybody is given the day off.

And as I thought about how the season was going, four things came to mind.

Conclusion #1. *Admit it, Brown, you have become totally obsessed*. Now I knew when I started taking notes about what it was like to coach Little League, I was taking all this a bit more seriously than I should. After all, coaching should be fun, not something you chart like the performance of your favorite stock. And when I starting shuffling index cards and plotting strategy instead of paying attention in staff meetings at work, I knew I might have gone too far. However, what will be forever known as "the thirty-one-page fax" proved it once and for all.

It started innocently enough. I had to go out of town for a couple of days and while I was gone, we were scheduled to play a game. No problem. That's why they have assistant coaches.

However, one of the reasons assistant coaches are often assistants is that they don't want all the grief and aggravation that comes from being in charge. They don't want to have to deal with the parents, make all the phone calls, and worry about how to deal with obnoxious colleagues. In short, whenever possible, they want to avoid the headaches that come with coaching, and one of the biggest headaches is figuring out who is going to hit where and what position they are going to play. You can't let the kids decide, because everybody always wants to play first base and hit cleanup.

Frank Roman, who served as my primary assistant, was pretty aggressive when it came to dealing with his son, but he took a different approach with everyone else. He didn't want the hassle of telling anybody "no." Frank asked if I could fill out the lineup before I left. That way he could blame everything on me if somebody was unhappy.

No problem, I said. I'll make out the lineup before I go. But I got backed up at work, and then they moved my flight up so I didn't have a chance to drop off the lineup before I left.

There was still no problem, though. Technology is a wonderful thing. I'd make out the lineup on the plane and fax it to Frank when I landed.

So far, so good.

Where I ran into trouble was the way I made out the lineup. I did it as I always did—with a myriad of options. After all, you never knew which kids would show up or who would ask to play where. (Whenever possible, I let the kids play where they wanted. While their initial responses were always "first base" and "cleanup," their second requests were usually more reasonable.)

So, I prepared not one lineup but seven, and not one defensive configuration but four. I was just trying to cover every possibility. The result was that the fax ended up being eleven pages long. I still haven't heard the end of it. It comes up at every coaches meeting. "Did you hear about the time

Brown was going away on a business trip, and sent this *thirty-one-page* fax that outlined what his assistant coach was supposed to do?"

Conclusion #2. *This sure is taking a lot of time.* I had known about the two games and a practice a week, but I hadn't counted on all the phone calls I would have to make in between.

Every time it rained I had to call ten kids to say the game/practice had been canceled, and tell them when the makeup would be. Then there were the calls to tell everyone when team pictures would be taken, when our end-of-the-season party would be held, and/or to explain that the game we scheduled for Tuesday would be held Thursday instead because the other team couldn't make it. By the time I had called everyone on the team, forty-five minutes had passed, and my left ear—the one I hold the phone to—hurt.

Why did it take so long? Because during each phone call I had to repeat the message at least twice and often three times.

If you have ever called a house where children over the age of two live, you'll understand. The kids always answer the phone. That makes sense. Odds are the call is for one of them. (Since the phone in our house never rings for me, I don't answer it either. I haven't ever since Peter turned four.)

The problem is that you are never quite sure, when you are talking to a kid, if the message is registering. All you hear is "Uh-huh, uh-huh, uh-huh, thanks. Good-bye." So, after telling the kids on my team that the time for practice had been changed, or whatever, I always asked to speak to "Mom, Dad, or anyone else who's there who's a bit older than you," to make sure at least one other person in the house got the message. Invariably, I'd be passed to an older (read ten-year-old) sibling, and I'd go through the whole routine again. More often then not the ten-year-old would listen to the whole message, then yell, "Mom," and once his mother picked up the phone, we'd start all over again.

I had thought I could short-circuit the process by asking for a parent whenever one of the kids on the team answered the phone, but that wasn't much better. Agam, or whoever, would just hand the phone over to his mother, and then stand at her elbow and ask every ten seconds, "What does he want? Has the game been changed? Are we going to have a practice?" And he would keep firing questions until his mother answered him—while I was still on the line—so the result was the same. Everything ended up being repeated at least twice.

Conclusion #3. *I am not here for your amusement—Part I.* Now as you have already figured out, I was taking all this Little League stuff too seriously, but a lot of the parents on my team were not taking it seriously enough. They thought nothing about coming to the game in the middle of the fourth inning and taking their son home—as Agam's father did once—because they thought it was too cold out, or because now was the perfect time to go get their child summer clothes. (That happened once too.)

And if I got more than two phone calls during the season explaining that little whoever couldn't make it because he had a cold, a choir practice, or a dentist appointment, that was a lot. I really didn't mind if a kid missed a game or practice. What bothered me was never knowing which kids would show up. Without knowing exactly who would be there, it was impossible to make out a lineup or figure out defensive positions ahead of time, and that meant every game was delayed "for just a few minutes more" while I waited to see who—if anyone—else would appear.

Conclusion #4. *I am not here for your amusement—Part*

II. More annoying than the parents who never bothered to tell you that their kids weren't coming were the ones who either left them at the games too long, or wanted me to double as their kid's baby-sitter and/or chauffeur.

One of your responsibilities, if you're coaching, is making sure that the kids on your team are constantly supervised. Among other things, that means you shouldn't leave after a practice or game until you're sure that everyone has a ride home and that they have been picked up.

Our games always lasted anywhere between ninety minutes and two hours, and I always scheduled practices to be an hour and a half long. I had told everyone at the beginning of the season what our schedule would be, and I also reminded the parents when they dropped their kids off what time the game or practice would end. (Very few people stayed for practices; and not everyone watched our games all the way through. Given the level of play, I'm not sure I blamed them.)

But no matter how many times I explained what our schedule was, somebody would forget, or come late, and there I'd be, fifteen, twenty, thirty minutes after everyone else was gone waiting with a kid—and often two—for the parent(s) to show up. The parents who were late—and there were two who seemed to make a point of showing up at least fifteen minutes late every time—never apologized, other than with a quick "I'm sorry." They seemed to figure that when I volunteered to coach, I was also volunteering to baby-sit.

The flip side of that was parents who assumed that their child had a God-given right to play Little League no matter what, and if they were unable to get them to the game—because, for example, they were going away for the weekend—then clearly it was up to me to pick up their kid at their house and then deposit him home at the end of the game. (Invariably, there would be a nanny there to watch him.)

127

What did all these annoyances add up to? Absolutely zero. Despite my complaints—invariably voiced at the dinner table when I knew I would have to call the kids to tell them that tomorrow's game was now a practice so there was no need to wear white pants—they were minor, petty, and a relatively small price to pay for the chance to coach. Despite all of my bellyaching, I was having a wonderful time.

In fact, I've already volunteered to be a head coach next year.

17

Game #6: *We're* the Team to Beat?

Traditionally during the All-Star break, fans, writers, and players project ahead and try to guess who is going to win the pennant. Well, no writers covered *our* games—we never even made *Holmdel Happenings*, a monthly newsletter mailed to everyone in town, let alone any of the three daily papers that cover the Jersey shore. The only fans who showed up at our games were parents, although an occasional grandparent or sibling could be seen standing outside the foul lines. And the only other players who had seen us were the ones we'd played and the few who'd shown up early for the game scheduled to follow ours.

Still, on the first day back at school following the Memorial Day weekend (All-Star break), Peter gave me some interesting news as he stepped off the school bus at 3:35 P.M.

"Guess what, Dad? *Everybody* at school says we're the best team in the league."

"Uh-huh."

"No, I mean it. That's what *everyone* told me during class, on the school bus, and everywhere."

Now *everybody* was pushing it a bit. I had a hard time picturing third graders being impressed by anything a lowly first or second grader might do. Peter's school ran K–3, with third graders enjoying the same kind of status that seniors receive in high school. Third graders were *seriously* cool and didn't acknowledge anyone else's existence.

But it did seem that the consensus among all the other first and second graders—and their coaches—was that we were the team to beat. That was flattering even if it didn't mean very much. After all, there were no World Series rings, trophies, or five-year contracts for the manager riding on the outcome of the season.

Still, this sudden consensus did set off some intriguing dominoes. For one thing, I noticed that a couple of coaches began copying they way we played the game, starting with how I designed our lineup.

Most teams alternated their good and bad hitters. It made sense, on the surface. If the kids you had batting ninth, tenth, and eleventh couldn't hit, that meant your team would go out easily in the innings where all three had to hit.

But the problem with going good hitter, good hitter, bad hitter, as most coaches did, was that you never really got a chance to build any momentum. Your two good hitters would get on, then there'd be an out, then two more players would get hits (which might produce a run or two), and then there'd be another out. With this kind of lineup, a good inning might produce 3 runs.

I preferred to bunch everyone who could hit at the top of

the order and take my chances with the bottom. By the time my first six or seven hitters had scored, the other team was often too demoralized to make a good play on a weak hitter.

I was convinced this strategy was a major reason we were doing so well, and a lot of coaches must have agreed. Following the break, I noticed three or four teams starting to group their best batters at the top of the lineup as well.

And at least one other team tried to copy our ninth batter play too. (It didn't work particularly well for them either, proving something I had known from the first day of practice. There's a reason Sparky Anderson and Tommy Lasorda are paid to manage and I'm not.)

The other interesting thing that happened was that a couple of people started coming to our games. It wasn't as if we had become Holmdel's version of a hot ticket—there were never more than forty watching no matter who or when we played— but I noticed that if our game was scheduled for 9:00 A.M., meaning it would end at ten-thirty or so, the teams scheduled to use the field after us started showing up around ten, whereas before Memorial Day, you'd be lucky if anyone got to the field before 10:28.

And what brand of baseball did they see? Could you tell at a glance we were the odds-on favorites? Were we so demonstrably better that we should have been playing against third and fourth graders? Was it clear to everyone that we had at least one, and possibly as many as four, potential major leaguers on our squad?

Hardly. Although in our sixth game they did see an unassisted triple play.

The game itself was boring. We had it won in the first inning when we jumped in front 8-0. Despite the big early lead, we weren't wonderful. At best we were adequate today. The only impressive thing about our offensive performance

131

was the fact that Justin Marconi hit five consecutive doubles to left field.

But the real reason we won had nothing to do with Justin's hitting. The fact was Tom Wilson's team was having an off-day.

Going into the game they had been 3-3, but there was no way you would have known that if this was the first time you had seen them play. Their fielding was atrocious. Basically anything we hit on the ground ended up being at least a double, since you could count on their infielders to miss it and on their outfielders to make a bad throw.

Things were even worse for Tom, an extremely competitive manager who knew where to draw the line. Although he made it a point to hold two practices a week and was not above keeping the kids after a game to go over something they had done wrong, *nobody* on his team could hit today. Even their best batters struck out at least once. In short, they looked like we did in the game we lost. Awful.

Where you really saw that was in their base running, and that's how the unassisted triple play came about.

Base running, even at best, was an adventure for all teams at this level. The reasons had to do with the age of the kids and their understanding (or lack of it) of the game. Let's take them one at a time.

Baseball is complicated. There are rules within rules within rules. For example, a foul ball always counts as a strike—except when it doesn't. If you hit a foul ball when you already have two strikes, nothing happens. As my four-year-old daughter would say, "It's a do over."

So you learn the rule about foul balls and the exception, and just when you think you have it straight, somebody tells you there is an exception to the exception. If you try to bunt with two strikes and the bunt goes foul, you're out. A bunted foul ball always counts as a strike no matter what.

It takes awhile to master the nuances of the game, and nowhere is that clearer than when it comes to running the bases. For example, we started with the basic understanding that if you are on base and the ball is hit on the ground, you should immediately head to the next base. That is, of course, unless you are on second and the ball is hit to the left side (that is, to the shortstop or third baseman). If either the shortstop or the third baseman catches the ground ball while you are running toward him, he can tag you out. So you want to make sure that neither can catch the ball, or that they have already thrown it to first before you start running.

As I said, this is pretty tricky stuff.

But explaining what to do as a base runner when the ball is hit on the ground was a piece of cake compared to telling the kids how to run the bases when the ball is hit in the air.

The basic rule is *go halfway*. If the ball is caught on the fly, the runner can't advance unless he first goes back to the base and tags up after the fielder has made the catch. If he leaves early, or fails to get back to the base before the ball, he's out.

So when a fly ball is hit you don't want to be too far off base, in case the ball is caught.

But if the ball falls in, you *do* want to run to the next base, so you don't want to be too close to your original base either.

Hence my advice: go halfway, and then wait to see if the ball is caught. But like all baseball rules this one, too, has an exception. The exception? If you are on base with two out, you should start running as soon as the ball is hit. Even if it's caught, you can't get into trouble. The catch would be the third out of the inning.

Now, all of this takes awhile to explain and even longer to learn, and most little kids are far better at getting their uniforms dirty by throwing dirt at one another than they are at mastering subtleties.

This changes later on. By the time the kids play in the third- and fourth-grade league, they understand the rules pretty well. For one thing they're self-selected. While virtually every parent in town signs up their first and second grader to play Little League, in much the same way that they require the kid to take piano and swimming lessons in the older grades, only the kids who really like the game come back. (While we had about 125 kids in the first- and second-grade register, only 85—a drop-off of about one third—would still be playing once they reached third grade.) And, of course, by the time they reach third grade they are a year or two older, and it's just easier to understand complicated things like baseball's rules.

At our level, however, you are never quite sure what they know and what they don't. Some kids, especially those like Peter or Agam who watched a lot of baseball, came to the league with a pretty good understanding of what was going on out on the field, but most didn't.

So I decided to spend a lot of time going over the rules and discussing strategy. You can do that, of course, by just sitting the kids down and lecturing them, but I never liked being lectured to as a kid. (More important, I have yet to meet any little kid who is capable of sitting still for an extended period.) So to keep this interesting, I worked the strategy in while we were doing other things.

For example, fielding drills are a staple of any baseball practice, whether you are playing tee-ball in the suburbs or pro ball in Yankee Stadium. And it works the same way in either case. A coach starts by hitting the ball to the third

134

baseman who throws it to first, then he hits one to the shortstop who throws to first, and so on.

We did that too, except I would invent situations before I hit the grounders.

"Okay, Wei, you're playing third, there's one out and a man on first." Then I'd hit him a ground ball and see where he'd throw it. Second base would be the preferred choice but first was also okay. At this level you took an out wherever you could get one.

We did the same thing with base running. I'd put a kid on first base and have another at the plate, and then I'd hit a ground ball to the infield—or a fly to the outfield—and the runners would have to figure out what they were supposed to do. At the same time the fielders would be trying to figure where *they* should make the play.

There were a couple of nice things about doing the drills this way. First, the kids stayed interested.

A dry discussion of what to do in a specific situation can become boring pretty quickly. However, the same situation, when people are running and a ball is coming your way, holds your attention.

Second, we were creating situations that forced the kids to look at the play from two different angles. If you were the fielder, you had to figure out what the runner was going to do as part of deciding what you should do with the ball. And when you were running, you had to look at the play from the fielder's perspective. Was he likely to get to the ball? Once he got there, what would he do next?

On routine plays, like a man on first and one out, there weren't a whole lot of options for either the infielder picking up the ground ball or the runner on first. But once the kids had mastered the basics, we moved on to more complex situations such as "man on second, nobody out." (The reason it's

135

more complicated is that the man on second isn't "forced" to run on a grounder since there's nobody on first base who wants to go to second.)

By the time the All-Star break rolled around, my kids had a pretty good idea of what to do on the base paths. Specifically, they knew what to do when they were on base and someone hit a fly ball. That was no small achievement, as you'll see in a minute.

For some reason, what to do as a beginner when the ball is hit in the air and you are on base is the most confusing thing to kids who are new to baseball. So we spent a lot of time on going halfway, and questions about what to do when the ball was hit in the air became a staple of my version of "Jeopardy."

The kids on my team, like most little kids everywhere, tend to be extremely competitive. That was something I tried to take advantage of in trying to explain how to play the game. So, for example, instead of lecturing them on how something should be done out in the field, I tried to turn everything into a game like "Jeopardy."

In our version of "Jeopardy," I'd give a specific kid, say Takeshi, a situation: "You're on second, there are two out, and the ball is hit high in the air. What do you do?" Then everybody else on the team would hum the "Jeopardy" theme, and Takeshi would have until we got all the way through it to give his answer. In this case, the correct response would be "start running the moment the ball is hit." Since there are two outs, if the fielder catches the ball, the inning will be over anyway so there is no reason to stay close to the base.

The combination of practicing specific situations, "Jeopardy," and the fact that we were continuing to play the games—and the kids continued to watch games on TV—

136

allowed us to do a decent job running the bases. We hit into very few double plays and no triple plays.

That couldn't be said for Tom's team.

Triple plays are rare. They happen on average about once a year in the big leagues. But the way we pulled ours off, you would have thought it was an everyday occurrence.

It happened in the fourth inning when we were comfortably ahead 11-2. (As the season went on, the scores got progressively lower as the kids got better at defense.) Tom's first two batters reached base with clean singles up the middle. That in itself was a bit surprising, since they were among the worst players on his team, the last two in the batting order.

The fact that they were inexperienced helps to explain what then happened.

The next batter hit a medium fly ball to center field. But instead of waiting to see if the ball would be caught, as my kids knew to do by now, both runners took off as soon as the ball left the bat. They shouldn't have. It turned out to be an easy fly ball that Peter, who is not above showing off, caught one-handed.

By the time the ball hit Peter's glove, the runner from second was almost to third and the runner from first had just about reached second.

Now a medium fly ball to center field in Shea Stadium means that it probably traveled about 330 or 340 feet from home plate. In Little League, a medium fly ball to center means it went about 25 feet beyond second base.

I always had my outfielders play deep because I'd learned the hard way that it is easier for them to move in to catch a fly ball than it is for them to backpedal. So on the fly to center, Peter was moving in as he made the catch. After he did, he kept on running and touched second base for the second out.

By this time the runner on first was totally confused. He knew the ball had been caught and he knew that meant he should do something, but it was clear from the look on his face that he couldn't remember what that something was. Compounding his problem was the fact that everyone on his team was yelling "Go back, go back!" But you could see that he didn't know if that meant he should go back to first base or return to second, where he had almost been when Peter caught the ball.

So the base runner did the only thing he could: he froze. Peter kept running and tagged him for an unassisted triple play.

For the first thirty seconds after he had done it, I doubt if there were more than six of us who knew what had just happened. Most everyone had seen the catch and Peter tag the runner. They'd just assumed it was a double play. They were shocked when Peter started running toward the dugout, exchanging high fives with Agam at short and Michael Roman at first, who knew exactly what he had done.

Eventually everybody figured it out and for the first time all season, I saw a unanimous display of good sportsmanship. Everybody, including the parents on Tom's team, started applauding.

Peter was unfazed. Sure it was an unassisted triple play, but what was the big deal? He could do this sort of thing all the time, he said.

Whatever comeback thoughts Tom's team might have had disappeared with the triple play. We held on to win 13-4.

We were now 4-1-1.

18

Game #7: Another Tie

I'm still not sure what happened.

One moment, we were comfortably ahead. The next, there were fourteen adults standing around home plate pointing fingers and trying to outyell one another.

The result? Total confusion and another tie game. And I am still trying to figure out what went wrong.

It started simply enough. We took the field against Bob's team, which was 0-7, and got them out one-two-three in the top of the first. No surprise there. By this point in the season our defense was extremely good—if unorthodox. It had taken me awhile, but I had finally figured out a way for everyone to play three innings in the outfield and three in the infield.

As I've said, one of the things I hated most about win-at-all-costs coaches was that they *always* batted their worst kid last and played him in right field for the entire game. I had

139

very few preconceived notions about what I would do once I became a coach, but one thing I knew for sure was that *nobody* was going to play right field the entire game. I wanted to make sure everyone got experience playing all over the field.

My solution? I created the "buddy system." Here's how it worked.

I took the kids on our team and paired them off on the basis of ability. Michael Roman and Bobby Foley were both good fielders who hit a lot of home runs so they became a team. Takeshi and Wei were solid, if unspectacular performers, so I put them together, and so on down the line. (It won't come as any surprise to learn that I matched Justin Marconi and Michael Goodman.)

Once everyone was assigned a partner (their "buddy"), I explained to them how our defense would work. One half of the pair (say, Tommy Foley) would start the game in the infield, in this case at third base, while his buddy (Stevie Moreno) would begin in the outfield (right center). They'd stay in those positions for the first half of the game. Then in the fourth inning they'd switch. Stevie would move to third, and Tommy would go to the outfield.

The buddy system accomplished a few things. It gave the kids practice playing both infield and outfield. Regardless of what the killer coaches thought, I was going to take the "instructional" part of Instructional Little League seriously. I didn't want Wei to know how to play just third base at the end of the season.

Second, moving them around kept the kids from getting bored. If you're playing first base or catcher, you have to stay awake. The catcher has to be ready every time the pitcher throws, and the first baseman is going to be involved in every infield play.

However, if you're out in left field, where two balls might

come your way in the course of a six-inning game, things can get mighty dull. And, invariably, you'll be starting to doze off just as someone hits a line drive over your head.

But while it was nice to try to keep the kids involved in the game and teach them more than one position, I still had to figure out how to rotate everyone in such a way that it wouldn't cost us too much. I still wanted to win a couple of games and that wasn't going to happen if I played Justin Marconi at first base. I could see Justin bending over to pick up a worm as the batter was barreling down the first base line, and one of my infielders had just thrown over to first. Collisions and bloody noses would be probable, victories would not.

It took a couple of games, but I finally worked out a system that made me—and the kids—happy. Our best fielders (Bobby, Agam, Michael Roman, Peter, Takeshi, and Wei) would always be up the middle or at first base, since those were the most pivotal positions. We'd take our chances elsewhere.

The system worked just fine. Michael and Bobby could be counted on to catch most balls thrown to first. Peter and Agam did a good job of backing up the other outfielders on balls that weren't hit to them in center field, and Takeshi and Wei could handle just about anything no matter where they played.

So when we got Bob's team out "three up, three down" in the top of the first it was unusual, but not unprecedented. It was unusual because it was very hard at this level to expect the kids to make three good defensive plays in a row. But it wasn't unprecedented because the kids' fielding was getting consistently better.

In the beginning of the year, we might have retired the side in order every other game, but as the season wound down you could depend on us doing it at least once, or twice, every game. Here we had done it early. Who knew? Maybe this would be the game where we held the other side scoreless. Shutouts were even rarer than triple plays.

In our half of the first we scored a couple of runs, and quite frankly, I stopped paying a lot of attention.

In our early games I could have told you what had happened on each and every play. But as the season progressed I became less hyper. Instead of being obsessively focused on each pitch, with a scowl permanently etched onto my face, I actually began to have fun. Invariably when we played, it was a bright spring day. The air was clean, and I was watching a bunch of kids—one of whom was mine—playing baseball. Or trying to. In short, a remarkable transformation had occurred. Once I got over my fear of losing every game, I actually started enjoying being a Little League manager.

And since I was having fun, I stopped tracking the score as closely as I had, and in this case, that turned out to be a big mistake.

In and of itself, my not knowing the score wasn't fatal. Since the coaches have enough to do, it's traditional for one parent on each team to serve as official scorer during the game.

In the big leagues, the term official scorer has some significance. He decides whether a hard-hit ball that bounces off someone's glove should be called a hit or an error, and he determines who should be the winning pitcher and who is entitled to the save. He is also the person responsible for preparing the box scores you see in the paper every morning.

In Little League, the position was both more and less important. Less, because at our level there are no official statistics to keep. We don't have batting champions, or Gold Glove or Cy Young award winners, so there is no need to rule whether something was a hit or an error—everything was called a hit—or to keep track of who was the best pitcher in the league. (That distinction, by definition, would have to go to the coach whose team had the best record.)

But even though we didn't keep official statistics, being the scorer was much more important for us than it was for the pros. In the big leagues, umpires are charged with making sure nobody bats out of order. They are also the folks who keep the official score. (The numbers on the scoreboard are just there for the convenience of the fans.)

So keeping score in Little League could be a big deal, especially if the coach (i.e., me) has stopped paying attention to whether his team is ahead by 1 run or 3. (I always had a pretty good idea of what the score was even if I had stopped writing it down on a piece of paper.)

Michael Roman's father usually kept score for us. And the way it worked was relatively straightforward. Before the game, and often just seconds before the game began, I would scribble a lineup on an index card or the back of an envelope. (As I said, I always waited until the last second because my kids had a habit of showing up late.)

Frank would translate my scribbles onto the official scorecards we were supposed to use. (Don't ask me why. Nobody ever collected them or even looked at them once the game was over.)

Once all the names and starting positions were recorded, Frank would meet with the official scorer of the other team and swap information. This way both official scorers had the same information before the game began. The two of them were then supposed to make sure that everybody played the field, and not only batted, but in the right order.

Through the first six games, the system worked just fine, but for some reason it broke down here.

Part of the reason was that it was incredibly hot. It's hard to pay attention when you feel like you are moving in slow motion, and you're constantly walking over to the dugout to steal sips from the kids' Gatorade bottles.

Another reason was that we were expected to win. After all, Bob's team had lost every game and we had been playing well. Neither Frank Roman nor Lisa Price, who was keeping score for Bob's team, had any reason to expect that things were about to change.

But the biggest reason was that both teams kept going to nine batters every time they hit, and the ninth batter rule, which had long plagued my kids (and me), was giving the official scorers fits as well.

While the ninth batter rule said the inning could end with someone stepping on home plate while holding the ball, it also stated it could end with a runner being tagged out as he rounded the bases.

When that happened, confusion was bound to result because if anyone touched the plate before the runner was tagged out, his run would count. So if you were the official scorer, you had to look at two places at once—at home plate, to see who had scored, and out on the field, to see exactly when the tag had been made.

At the end of each inning, the two official scorers were supposed to meet and compare notes on the number of runs scored, and who scored them, but it just didn't happen today. By the time they each had sorted out what had happened in the previous inning, the next one was under way.

As I said, even once I stopped being obsessive about managing, I always tried to keep track of the score myself. But between ensuring that everybody stayed in position when we were on defense, and pitching when we were up, I was almost always off by a run or two. I did know this game was closer than I'd expected. Bob's team was playing its best game of the year on offense *and* defense, and my kids all looked as if they had stayed up too late the night before. Still, as we headed into the top of the sixth, I figured we were ahead by a couple of runs.

As our kids took the field, I yelled over to Frank, "What's the score?"

"Fifteen-fourteen, us," he said.

Frank's counterpart Lisa was heard from about a second later. "No, that's not right. *We're* ahead by one."

Frank and Lisa met behind the batting cage and probably could have figured out what the real score was, but parents from both teams started coming over to "help out." The more parents, the more points of view. The yelling started shortly thereafter.

The only thing that became clear, during the ten minutes of discussion that fourteen supposedly rational grown-ups decided to conduct at the top of their lungs, was that nobody knew for sure how many runs had scored in the first, third, and fourth innings—the three times that either team, or both, had sent nine kids to the plate.

As I said, I had no idea what the actual score was. And I figured my getting involved in the "discussion" wasn't going to help any. But I did have a thought. The kids might know the score. After all, the odds were pretty good that they had been paying attention.

It turned out I was half right. They *had* been paying attention—to how they *individually* had been doing. About the *team's* performance they were a whole lot less certain. But if you asked them, each kid on my team could tell you exactly how he had done that day.

Peter: "I singled in the first and second. Grounded out in the fourth, and doubled in the fifth.

Takeshi: "Single, single, single, and single.

145

Agam: "Home run, fly out, single, triple."

And so it went down the line.

Initially, I had thought it would be possible to reconstruct at least our score by adding up the kids' performances, but I quickly learned that that was not going to be the case. It seemed the kids had a tenuous grasp on reality.

While they could tell you where they ended up on base after they hit the ball, they weren't sure of anything else about the play. For example, I knew for a fact that when Michael Roman said he'd singled in the first, that wasn't what had happened. He had indeed ended up on first base, but only after the shortstop who'd fielded his ground ball threw to second, forcing Bobby Foley, who had been on first. You couldn't take the kids' recollections at face value.

By the time I figured that out, all the yelling had started to subside. Fifteen minutes after Frank had called out "fifteen-fourteen, us," it was clear that we were never going to know what the "real" score was. I met with Bob and we decided to do the only thing we could. We said the score was tied 14-14 at the end of five, and we continued the game.

We held them scoreless in the top of the sixth, but they returned the favor in our half. While Wei, Tommy Foley, and Justin each hit the ball hard, somebody on Bob's team managed to catch it each time.

Neither Bob nor I wanted to play extra innings.

The result? Another tie.

To this day, I meet parents and members of either team who tell me the game shouldn't have ended that way. Either we (or they, depending on who is doing the talking) really won 15-14. But what can you do? I always ask. Welcome to the joys of Little League.

19

Game #8: The Problem with Girls (The *Real* Problem Is Not Having Enough of Them on Your Team)

A confession.

I was raised in an open-minded home, educated at public schools in the tolerant Northeast, and was an American history major at a good co-educational liberal arts college where the history department was chaired by an avowed Marxist. I worked on the college newspaper, which had offices on the fourth floor of the student center, just down the corridor from where the women's rights group on campus was based. And on more than one occasion the editors (some of whom were female) and members of the women's collective, were known to go drinking at the campus hang a block away. Everyone got along just fine.

My wife, at different points in our marriage, has made more money than I have and that hasn't caused any problems. (It caused her to buy a sports car, but that's another story.) Since we're in the same business, it's very easy to judge that she is just as good as I am at what she does, and no, she didn't change her name after we got married. (The only problem with that decision is that my mother-in-law keeps addressing birthday cards and the like to my wife by writing "Mrs. Paul B. Brown" on the envelope. She doesn't want the mailman to think her daughter, who still has her "maiden" name, is living in sin.)

I have been known, on occasion, to do laundry, wash dishes, and cook (although I'm not crazy about any of these—but then, again, either is my wife).

I have worked for women, and have had women work for me. Some of them were fine, others were jerks, which means that they were no different than the men I've worked for, and the ones who have worked for me.

And while I don't eat quiche, think there are definite differences between the sexes (for which I—and my hormones—are extremely glad), and believe it's perfectly all right to impose strength requirements before someone—male or female—can work for the police or fire department, I am not the type of guy Alan Alda or Phil Donahue will hate on sight.

So what's the confession? Simply this: for the first thirty-three years of my life, I believed that letting girls play Little League was one of the most stupid ideas ever proposed on God's green earth.

Then my daughter was born.

Pre–Shannon Rachel Peck Brown, my thinking on the matter was pretty straightforward. Since there are no women in the big leagues, it just didn't make any sense to have girls play Little League. There was no future in it.

Yes, I knew that 99.99999 percent of the boys who dream of playing pro ball as they stand out on a Little League field are never going to go on to the majors. But for that other 0.00001 percent, the dream can, and does, come true. There are literally dozens of pro baseball players who began their careers in Little League.

While boys face daunting odds, their chances of playing pro ball are far better than they are for any girl. Ergo, girls shouldn't play Little League.

I concede my logic was fuzzy, but that's how I felt and I was adamant about it. (This is in keeping with my own personal motto: often wrong but never in doubt.) Despite my good liberal upbringing and education, my position was firm. Girls shouldn't play Little League. Period. Full stop.

And then my daughter entered the world, and my feelings promptly took a 180-degree turn.

If someone had told me while I was holding Shannon in the delivery room that "girls can't play Little League," I would have very calmly handed my daughter back to my wife and decked him. Who are you, buddy, to tell *my* little girl (who you'll remember is now three or four minutes old) what she can and cannot do?

I could picture myself saying something brilliant like "so there" as my right hook caused my daughter's challenger to hit the floor. For the record I have not been involved in a fistfight since I was seven and I lost that one. Still, I was willing to fight again on behalf of my just-born daughter, who, while already remarkably advanced at the age of seven minutes, probably still wasn't ready to face overhand pitching.

The township's position was not quite as militant as mine.

Holmdel offered girls two choices. They could play softball in an all-girl league if they wanted, or they could play Little League with the boys.

The vast majority of girls played softball. For many it was a question of boys being "yucky." They simply wanted to

149

keep their interaction with the nonfairer sex to a minimum. They also just wanted to be with their friends, and most of their friends were playing softball, not baseball, so they'd play softball, too.

As we went through the index cards on draft night, only 3 of the 125 or so kids who would play in the first- and second-grade league were girls. But all three ranked in the top 10 percent in ability, and each girl would end up being the highest-rated player on her team. In fact, Jennifer Johansen was *the* highest-rated player in the entire league.

There were three reasons I was not surprised.

First, if you're going to be different than your peers—and if you're a girl, opting to play Little League with the boys definitely made you different—you (or your parents) had to be pretty self-confident. Without examining the psychological makeup of a seven-year-old too closely, signing up for Little League told the world that you had to feel you could more than hold your own in this strange environment. The ratings of Jenny, Jamie, and Julie ("J" names were very popular back in the early 1980s) proved that their confidence was justified.

Second, there was that old saw that said girls matured earlier than boys. I'm still not convinced that is always true, but it certainly was the case here. All three girls were much taller and more muscular than Peter, even though all four had been born during the summer of 1982.

And finally, you had to figure that, if the girls were going to be deliberately different, their parents were going to be supportive. (As a corollary, my personal rule of thumb is that any time you meet a girl with a boy's name, like Jamie, you can be pretty sure one of the parents—probably the father—wanted a boy.)

In either case, that meant that someone had probably been

working with the girls for a while, teaching them how to run, hit, and throw.

Given all this, I was hoping that I would get at least one girl on my team. That put me in the majority, but it was far from an overwhelming one.

A lot of the coaches just didn't want girls on their team, no matter how highly they were rated. Either they held my pre-Shannon position that having girls play Little League was dumb, or they were sexist. In either case, it was clear that they hadn't thought the matter through. Why would you *willingly* turn down one of the few good players in the league, unless he or she was a discipline problem? (None of the girls were.)

But the fact was that about a third of the guys—Joe being the most vocal among them—just didn't want a girl on their team.

You know, of course, what happened. I didn't get any of the three girls. By the time I got around to picking in the draft (remember, I went last) they were all gone. Joe got Jennifer Johansen, whose high rating was absolutely correct. She was far and away the best player in the league.

Now had the Holmdel Youth Athletic Association been a "B" movie, which I have to admit it resembled at times, Joe would have kicked and screamed about getting "stuck" with Jennifer Johansen and would have banished her to the outfield all season long. Then, through an amazing string of coincidences that only seems to happen in Hollywood, she somehow would be involved in *the* pivotal play, in *the* pivotal game of the year. Jenny, of course, would save the day and be carried off the field on the shoulders of her teammates. In the final scene you'd see Joe, with his arm around Jenny's shoulders, saying "You're all right, kid."

151

Well, Frank Capra didn't write the script. Joe grimaced when he got Jenny, and gave a dirty look to those of us who had been praising her athletic abilities, me among them. (Peter had invited Jenny to his seventh birthday party, which we held in a local bowling alley, and she rolled the highest score in all three games.)

By the end of Joe's first practice, Jenny was playing first base, and during the first exhibition game she was batting cleanup. She stayed in both places all year long.

In our eighth game I got a chance firsthand to see how good she really was.

How good was she?

Very.

Peter learned that the hard way his first time up. He took one of my outside pitches and hit a line drive about six feet off the ground toward right field. Now, Peter did that a lot. We had spent a lot of time trying to work on, as the pros say, "hitting the ball where it's pitched." Translation: if the ball is outside, a right-handed hitter like Peter should try to hit it to right field; if it's inside, he should try to hit it to left. The advantage is that you can hit the ball a lot harder if you hit it where it's pitched. And this one, as baseball announcers are apparently required to say at least once a game, was "hit a ton."

In every other game we played, a ball hit like that would have sailed over the first baseman's head and rolled forever down the right field line for a home run.

Here? Jenny jumped up and caught it. One down.

Her defense was consistent throughout the game. One of the great adventures in Little League is the basic, everyday grounder hit to an infielder. This routine play is filled with suspense, danger, and even intrigue. Will the fielder get to the ground ball before it scoots into the outfield? If he does,

152

will he field it cleanly? And, if he accomplishes both those things—and as our scores indicate, that didn't happen a lot—then comes the biggest mystery of all: will the first baseman be able to catch the throw?

Even at their best the kids' throws to first were none too good. They either bounced, often a couple of times, before they got there—when you are seven, the distance from shortstop or third to first base can look 100 yards long—sailed to the right or left, or took off in the general direction of the parking lot behind first base.

However, if the ball was thrown anywhere near Jenny, she managed to haul it in.

At bat she was no less impressive. The word on the grapevine was that Jenny could hit, so I had everyone playing deep. But even though our outfielders were a good thirty feet further back than they played for anyone else in the league, she managed to hit two balls over Agam's head in center field. Both went for home runs. Fortunately for us there was only one person on base when Jenny hit the first one, and nobody on when she hit the second—a ball that probably traveled 200 feet from home plate. Pretty impressive for an eight-year-old—of either sex. Still, it only cost us one run.

And that, in microcosm, was the problem with Joe's team and, to a lesser extent, with the two other teams that had girls. With the exception of the girls, there really was nobody else the coach could count on.

Part of that was the way the draft was set up, and part of it was fate.

Because the players were supposed to be evenly distributed based on ability, if you got a highly rated player like Jenny as your first pick, the second player you received would be nowhere near as good. So while Joe got Jenny, the number-one player in the league, he had to wait until everyone else had picked before he got another player. In theory, his second pick should have been the twelfth best player in the league.

It didn't always work out that way. Low-rated players had a habit of becoming stars—because they were rated incorrectly; grew 4 inches and put on 15 pounds from when they were rated in June and the time Little League began the following April; or because they just practiced a lot. The converse could also hold true. Highly rated players could turn out to be duds—because they had been overrated; got big early and lost their advantage as other kids caught up with them; or, as happened in a surprisingly large number of cases, simply because they peaked in first grade.

But in Joe's case the system worked the way it was supposed to. With the exception of Jenny, his team was just average. They had come into the game 3-4. They left 3-5.

We were workmanlike. After Peter lined out to Jenny, Takeshi singled, Agam singled, Bobby doubled Takeshi in. Michael Roman then struck out. (Hitting home runs in our three previous games apparently had gone to his head; he swung as hard as he could and came within waving distance of the ball.) Wei singled Agam in and we were ahead 3-0. Jenny retired Tommy Foley by catching his popup, which came down on the third base side of the pitcher's mound, then fielded the ground ball Michael Goodman hit between first and second and beat him to the base.

By the time we went to bat in the second inning, both the kids and I were doing everything in our power to make sure that Jenny wouldn't be involved on defense.

I started pitching all right-handed hitters inside to try to force them to pull the ball toward short and third (and away from Jenny). And a couple of kids—Bobby Foley in particular—went beyond my not-so-subtle strategy.

When Bobby got up to hit in the second inning, he changed

his swing. Instead of cocking the bat back, he only brought it back halfway, and instead of swinging, he twisted his body toward third base and sort of punched at the ball. There was just no way Bobby was going to let Jenny get him out. And she didn't. Bobby's unorthodox swing produced a base hit that landed just beyond second base.

Did all these machinations pay off?

It probably ended up a wash.

While we did manage to keep Jenny involved in a minimum of plays, all the fiddling around with our batting stances, and with where I pitched the ball, probably minimized the effectiveness of our offense. We only scored 11 runs, about 6 below our season average.

It didn't really matter. Our defense was good enough, and with the exception of Jenny's hitting, nobody else on Joe's team did very much.

Final score: 11-5, Good Guys.

Only two more games to go.

20

Game #9: Anticipation

Pro athletes have a saying they dust off every time a big series is coming up, or people start looking forward to a crucial game scheduled for later in the season.

"You got to play them one at a time," they always say. "We have to stay focused on the task at hand."

It's a wonderful line, even if it's almost never true. Athletes are more or less like the rest of us, and everyone likes looking ahead. (My kids start making out their Christmas lists somewhere around Labor Day.)

Still, the idea behind what has now become a cliché is sound. If you don't win the contests leading up to *the big game*, the big game itself won't mean a thing. A battle of two undefeated college football teams late in the season is exciting, a game between a team that is 11-0 and one that is 7-4 (because it lost the games leading up to the big one) isn't.

To make sure that they are not guilty of looking ahead, the players say they "can't watch the scoreboard" (to see how their potential opponent is doing) and must "stick with the things that got us here," and . . . you get the idea.

I started thinking about all this as we got ready to play game #9. The reason? I could have cared less about the game at hand. I was more concerned about the final game of the season, which, through a scheduling fluke, would decide who had the best record in the league.

After eight games our 5-1-2 put us ahead. In second place was the team coached by Scott, the real estate developer turned venture capitalist, whose kids were 6-2. Nobody else was even close.

Assuming we both won our ninth game—and in violation of all the clichés I was assuming just that—the standings going into the final day of the season would look like this:

Us: 6-1-2 (a .857 winning percentage; you don't count ties).
Scott: 7-2-0 (.778).

If we beat Scott, we'd be the league champions. If we lost, the title would be his. True, we both would have two losses, but one of ours would have been to Scott, so common sense said you'd have to cede the championship to him. Besides, the numbers would give you no choice. Scott's winning percentage (.800) would be better than ours (.750), if he won.

Now, have I mentioned in the last five minutes that there was *no* league championship? There were *no* official standings and all of this worrying about who would end up as league "champion" was just silly posturing on the part of Scott (who had done exactly the same arithmetic I had), me, and everyone else who was anticipating the big game. It was nuts. The reality was there simply was *no* championship to worry about.

Did that stop me? Of course not.

As we got set to play game nine, I was mentally double-checking the strategy I had employed all season long to see if there were any weaknesses that Scott could exploit. To say that I was distracted going into this game would be like calling Henry Kissinger a high school graduate: it was true, but it understated the situation by just a bit.

Fortunately for me, the kids were oblivious to all my concerns. They weren't looking ahead. They went out and played a solid game and did it with very little help from their distracted coach. It was as if they were on auto-pilot. But by this point in the season that made sense.

For one thing, they knew what the defense would be. They knew they would play three innings in the infield and three in the outfield, and by now, the exact positions they would play were set as well. Stevie Moreno always played second base or right center, as did his "buddy" Tommy Foley. So it was simply a matter of telling Tommy and Stevie who would start where.

The more obnoxious kids, my son among them, didn't even wait to be told. They worked it out among themselves. Sometime before the game, often at school, Peter and Agam would divide up the six innings between them. They figured, and rightly so, that I didn't care when either of them played shortstop or center, as long as they each played three innings at both positions.

Knowing that, they designed some weird combinations (Peter at short in the first, second, and sixth may have been the most bizarre) but they always made sure that their time in the infield and outfield was evenly split. It got to the point where I didn't even bother checking with them to see who would be where. I let it come as a surprise.

When it came to the batting order there were no surprises. After the second game, the lineup became fixed with Peter, Takeshi, and Agam at the top of the order, and Justin,

Tommy, and Michael at the bottom. By the third game the kids had the order memorized and I rarely had to remind anybody when he was up.

So, the fact that my concentration was elsewhere during this game didn't really hurt us. The kids knew what they were supposed to do—and they did it. To them this game was just as important as all the rest. As I've said, to them *all* games were a matter of life and death while they were playing them, and instantly forgettable once they were over.

That took awhile to get used to, but eventually I figured out why they thought that way: from a kid's perspective, grown-ups think too much.

While an adult can spend hours pondering what might happen in the days ahead (Will he call me? Would she go out with me if I asked?), kids can't. Their frame of reference when it comes to time is much shorter. Lunch can seem like it's weeks away, when you are hungry at ten-thirty. And why would you want to waste time worrying about what could happen Saturday when there is a game today, or that huge rock over there that you can turn over to see what's underneath?

They weren't looking ahead. They were concentrating on today's game, and against a team that was pretty bad, they played well.

You saw that in our offense. We scored more runs than we had in a while—21—with the big blows coming from two unexpected sources: Michael Goodman and Tommy Foley.

Tommy's 3-hit performance is the easier of the two to explain. When Tommy swung the bat, it looked like a pendulum. He always started with the bat down around his ankles and brought it up in an arclike motion, until it ended up near his shoulders. I had tried working with him to see if we could even out his swing, and when that failed, I decided to employ the Justin Marconi rule of pitching and aimed at his bat, but

159

nothing worked. Either he kept swinging and missing, or on those rare occasions when he actually hit the ball, it went straight up.

Today, I finally figured out that what I had to do was pitch Tommy up high. Instead of trying to catch him early in his swing, I waited until the last minute. All of a sudden, Tommy looked like the second coming of Reggie Jackson.

I have no explanation at all for Michael Goodman's sudden flashes of brilliance.

Michael had spent the entire season swinging with his eyes closed. It worked the same way every time. I'd pitch; he'd shut his eyes and swing and (usually) miss.

I tried cajoling him, but that didn't work. I had his parents go out and buy him a Whiffle bat and ball and practice with him in their backyard, hoping that once he saw how easy it was to hit at home he'd start hitting in the games. I even let him throw a half-dozen balls at me so he could see that even if he was accidentally hit by the ball, it wouldn't hurt. (We used a regulation-size ball that had a squishy center, so that the kids couldn't get hurt by either a pitch, or a ball that took a bad hop.)

But despite all my efforts, Michael kept swinging with his eyes closed—until this game. For some reason, he tried batting with his eyes open his first time up and got a clean single to center. After that he was hooked. He kept his eyes open and got two more hits—which doubled his season total. You have never seen a happier kid in your life.

Tommy's and Michael's hitting coupled with adequate defense—both Peter and Agam dropped easy fly balls—made it possible for me to go through the motions.

Final score, 21-12.

The "championship" is next.

21

Game #10: Showdown

You knew from the start this game would be different. For one thing we had a crowd—of sorts. For another, all my kids showed up before the first pitch.

Let's take them one at a time.

I felt like I was being watched as I started laying out the equipment and placing the bases on the field thirty minutes before game time. It was a strange feeling and there could be, I thought, only one possible explanation. "Okay, Brown, the stress of managing a Little League team has finally gotten to you. You're imagining people are staring at you. Congratulations. You are officially paranoid."

When I looked up, I realized that wasn't the case, but rather something almost as odd was happening. There were two or three coaches, their sons, and a handful of other folks standing behind the batting cage waiting for the game to begin.

Now this had never occurred before. A coach never went to another coach's game. Their kids might, if their best friend was playing and neither "Full House" nor "Family Matters" was on TV that night. But coaches? Never. Nobody had that kind of time. It was hard enough to free up ten or fifteen hours a week to spend with your own team without worrying about what someone else was doing.

That had been the case all season long. Yet there were Mike, Bill, and Tom chatting away, waiting for our game to begin. What were they doing here?

They were casual about it when I asked. Oh, no big deal, they said. They were just curious to see who was going to win the championship.

The championship?

What championship?

"We don't have a championship game, remember?" I said, trying to downplay the significance of the game that I had been building up in my mind all season. "This is just the last game of the season. Next year, there are playoffs, trophies, all-star teams, and most valuable player awards. But this year it's just for fun, right?"

Yeah, well, maybe, they started to say, but just then I had to excuse myself. As I looked around, I saw another amazing thing. It looked like everyone on my team was here—a full thirteen minutes before someone would yell, "Play ball!" That may not sound like much to you, but for us, this, too, was a first.

All the weekday games were scheduled to begin at 6:00 P.M., and tonight's game was no different. What *was* different was that all my kids were now here and it was only 5:47.

162

During the first nine games, I was lucky if I had enough players by 6:05.

At the beginning of the season when I handed out the schedules, I asked that everyone try to show up at least fifteen minutes before the game—but no one ever did. If we could get everyone there even slightly ahead of time, I figured, we could have a pregame strategy meeting or work on one specific thing (like the ninth batter rule) before the start of the game. At the very least, it would give me a couple of minutes to prepare our lineup and defensive alignment.

But 6:00 P.M. is a difficult time to schedule anything—especially if you're a working parent who has to swing by the house, get your child into his uniform ("Mom, have you seen my cleats?"), and still try to get to the game on time. So I was lucky if I had everyone there by five or ten after six. But not today.

Maybe my constantly repeated "Please show up early for the next game" had finally sunk in.

Maybe the kids understood the importance of this game.

Maybe there was no traffic.

Whatever the reason, here it was a full thirteen minutes before game time and I had—when I counted—ten of my eleven players. Agam was missing.

This could be trouble. After all, Agam was our best player. Still (for us) it was early and I wasn't ready to start worrying yet. Agam often showed up late.

By 5:58, I was officially concerned. Yes, it *was* true that Agam often showed up late. But it was also true that he missed a lot of games. Peter was a good friend of Agam, they were in the same class at school and usually sat together at lunch, so I figured he might know something.

I turned to Peter and we started one of those conversations

that proves my theory about why children exist: kids are God's way of ensuring that their parents die off—it's His plan for population control.

I repeat the conversation in its entirety.

"Hey, Peter, was Agam in school today?"

"Yeah."

"That's odd. I wonder why he isn't here yet?"

"Oh, I forgot. He said I should tell you that he won't be able to make it tonight. He had to go somewhere with his family."

"*Aaggah!*"

So much for the defensive alignments I had worked out earlier based on the assumption that everybody would show up. (Agam was starting at short.) So much for the batting order I was happy with. (Agam was batting third.) Once again at the last minute I was forced to figure out who was going to play where.

Now, Scott, who was coaching the other team, never seemed to have any of these problems. His kids always showed up at least thirty minutes before every game. That gave everybody a chance to take a few swings and field some ground balls before things got under way.

More important, given my problems with Agam's attendance, Scott's key players never missed a game.

When it came to kids with lesser ability, it was a different story.

It seemed—and maybe it was my overactive imagination again—that whenever there was an important game at least one, and often two or three, of Scott's worst players failed to show. Maybe it was a coincidence, but it seemed to happen every time based on what I had seen and heard.

And it was no different here. Scott, like me, had eleven

players on his team. But today his versions of Michael Goodman and Justin Marconi were nowhere to be found.

The advantages of having your worst players call in sick are obvious. Just about every time he came up to hit, Michael Goodman made an out. If he wasn't there, it would mean better batters would get a chance to hit more often. The odds said they'd get more hits and make less outs than Michael. The result? More runs for us.

We'd have an advantage out in the field, too, if Justin wasn't there. A better fielder would be playing third base and left field, Justin's two positions. Whoever we put there was bound to catch more balls.

Did Scott deliberately tell his two worst kids not to show up? Probably not. But it was awfully convenient.

In any event, Scott had four good players present compared to my three, and each of his nine kids could play. I had ten kids in uniform and two of them would have forced Abner Doubleday to wonder whether inventing baseball had been a good idea.

I tried to convince myself that this was no big deal.

"Okay, you're starting at a disadvantage. But maybe things will work out all right."

And at the beginning of the game it looked like they just might. We were up first. Peter singled, Takeshi singled and Bobby Foley (moved up to third in the order, because Agam was not here) came up to bat.

Now Scott, as was his practice, had scouted our two previous games so he was well aware that Bobby could hit. He not only moved his outfielders back a good forty feet, he also moved his infielders back to the edge of the outfield grass.

It didn't matter. Bobby swung at my first pitch and hit the ball over the center fielder's head: 3-0 us. Still nobody out.

Life was looking pretty good, and then came the incident with the bat.

The moment Bobby crossed home plate, Scott came walking over from the third base dugout.

"Hey, Bobby," he said, reaching up to give a surprised Bobby Foley a high five. "Nice shot. You really tagged that one."

"Thanks."

"Can I take a look at your bat?"

"Sure."

Scott picked it up and saw that it was one that Bobby's parents had bought for him after Bobby complained, following our first practice, that the Little League bats we had been issued were too light. Bobby's bat weighed 29 ounces, a good 25 percent more than the ones used by the other kids.

"You sure this isn't too heavy for you?" Scott asked.

Now the answer to that was obvious. Bobby had just hit what in the pros would have been described as a "tape measure" home run. So it was clear that the bat wasn't too heavy for him. But Bobby, who is pretty quick, figured out the point of Scott's question.

"Can't I use it?"

Now that was a good question. While the answer was "probably yes," nobody knew for sure.

At the beginning of the season, all the coaches are given two bats for the kids to use. The bats are between six to eight inches shorter than the ones the pros use and can weigh up to 12 ounces less.

But while the league provides bats, it isn't mandatory to use them during the game. Kids are free to bring their own bats, but we had never discussed what size and weight they should be. All the coaches had agreed that we wouldn't let the kids use metal bats—we thought they were too dangerous—but after that, the question of what kind of bat to use was pretty open-ended.

The fact that Bobby used a bat far heavier than anyone else's hadn't been a problem—until now. And while Scott was quick to stress that he wasn't "complaining," just "curious," Bobby took that curiosity to mean that his heavier bat was giving him an unfair advantage over the other kids. If you were looking for an analogy you could say it was as if Bobby was using a fiberglass pole when everyone else jumped with a bamboo one in the pole vault.

Scott left after congratulating Bobby again, but the message had gotten through. His next time up, Bobby—on his own—went up to hit carrying one of the Little League–issued bats.

Now, I was never one of the world's best science students, but I do remember a little of what I was taught in high school physics. If two objects—say, baseball bats, each swung with equal force—hit balls moving at equal speeds, the heavier object will drive the ball farther every time. The ball hit with the lighter bat just won't go as far.

And you got proof of that Bobby's second time up. He swung just as hard as he had before, but this time the ball was caught in center field.

The "bat incident" was just a little thing, of course. But it was one in a series of little things, such as Scott's two worst players not showing up. It was just something else that gave him a slight edge. And while Bobby went back to using his own heavier bat his third time up (and promptly hit another home run), we had lost forever what he might have done his second time at bat.

Now I am quick to concede that all this might be sour grapes on my part, coupled with a healthy dose of paranoia. It is more than likely that Scott not only had a better team but was also a better coach.

You certainly could make that argument based on what was going on out on the field.

His team just kept besting us by a little bit each inning. In the top of the first, we scored 3 but they answered with 4. In the second, we got 3 but they got another 4. And while the third inning was our best of the game—we scored 6 runs—they promptly came back with 8. When their ninth batter came up, Michael Roman, who was playing center field instead of Agam, misjudged a fly ball that Agam probably (grumble, grumble) could have caught. The batter and both runners on base scored.

I had been fantasizing about this being a 1-run ballgame that would be decided in the last inning by my managerial brilliance. (True, I didn't know what form that genius would take, but hey, it was a fantasy.) But it was not to be. With fewer bad players and one additional good one, it quickly became clear to me that Scott would be able to turn what I had pictured as a no-holds-barred battle into a rout.

At the end of three they were ahead 16-12 and it was painfully obvious to just about everyone—me included, I'm afraid—that we were lucky to be that close.

Following the last game of the 1990 World Series, after the underdog Cincinnati Reds soundly thrashed the defending champion Oakland A's in four straight games, an unrepentant Dave Stewart, Oakland's best pitcher, said, "The best team didn't win." I had no such illusions.

It wasn't that we played badly. We didn't. Michael Roman's misplayed fly ball was the only major lapse on our part. It was just that we were, in a word, overmatched.

One play in the fourth inning brought it all home to me. We had scored 3 and were down by a run. The bases were loaded, there were 2 out, and Bobby Foley was up again. Here was our chance to set things right, I thought. If we could just jump out to a lead, maybe we'd be able to get a break or two and steal the game. By now I had given up thinking our superior talent or my managerial skill would win the game for us. I was now hoping for luck.

And this bases-loaded situation could provide it. If Bobby could just hit one hard, it was more than likely that we could take a 3-run lead. I threw the ball in slowly, waist high, right over the center of the plate.

Bobby did, indeed, hit it hard, but instead of swinging slightly under the ball as he usually did—which would have sent it soaring—he hit this one a bit above the center. The result was a sinking line drive that took off toward left field.

This still could be okay, I told myself as the ball headed toward third. Once it got to the outfield, who knew what could happen?

There was only one problem. The ball never got to the outfield.

It hit the ground at the feet of the third baseman, and for a moment I was thrilled. The toughest play for an infielder to make—whether you're eight or twenty-eight—is a line drive that bounces right in front of you. First, you have no time to react. Second, fielding it cleanly requires you to bend down and put your face directly in the path of the oncoming ball. Since the natural tendency is to turn your head when an object is coming directly at your face, most fielders look away and only end up making the catch by accident. Usually the ball just bounces off their glove and heads into the outfield.

But not here. Jason, Scott's third baseman, bent right down to get the ball and never flinched as it came toward his face. He fielded it cleanly and without hesitating, stepped on third for the final out of the inning. As his foot came down on the base, I realized our season was over. There was no way we were going to be able to come back after that. And we didn't.

Scott's team scored 5 in the bottom of the fourth to take a 6-run lead, and while we managed to cut it to 4 in the top of the fifth, that was as close as we'd come. We ended up losing by 7, 22-15.

It was over.

At the end of each game, we always made the kids line up and shake hands with the opposing team. Win or lose, you were supposed to say "good game" or words to that effect. As we lined up now, I must have looked more crestfallen than the kids. They were smiling and from their perspective they had good reason to. Not only had they played a good game but I had promised to take them out for all the pizza they could eat as soon as we put the equipment away.

As I watched them from the sidelines, smiling and shaking hands with everybody on Scott's team, I suddenly felt better. I realized there was no reason to be depressed. We had accomplished everything I had set out to do before the season began. I had wanted all the kids to have a good time, and just looking at them, you knew they had. I hadn't consigned anybody to be the permanent right fielder, and we had even managed to win a few games. There was nothing to be upset about.

Besides, wait till next year.

22

Extra Innings: An Epilogue of Sorts

Next year came too soon.

The lead-in, however, wasn't bad.

I agreed to coach soccer again—this time as a head coach—as Peter entered third grade that fall, and it was less awful than it had been in the past. For one thing, I finally understood the difference between a corner kick and a goalie kick, and to my complete surprise, I actually learned what being "offside" meant. (Don't ask. We don't have the time.)

All of this helped—a little. But only a little. In addition to its big Asian population, Holmdel also has a surprisingly large number of native Europeans, who have also been drawn to the township by Bell labs. While they always have their kids play basketball in the winter and baseball in the spring—because they want their children to be "true Americans"—it was easy to tell their hearts weren't in it. If you grew up playing cricket, it has to be awfully hard to watch your kid play baseball.

Ah, but football—what we here in the States call soccer—was another matter. Fathers with names like Wilhelm, Gunther, and Lars were always among the first to sign up to coach. They were thrilled to teach the kids the intricacies of the diamond defense and the like. Invariably, their teams turned in the best records.

We went 3-4-3 for the season, in my first year as a head soccer coach, and that was just fine with me.

Basketball, however, was a different matter.

The allocation of talent in basketball was a little fairer than it had been in baseball the year before. There were eight teams and the commissioner made sure that each got at least one highly rated third grader and one good fourth grader.

I got the highest-rated third grader, John Donovan, and the lowest-rated—of the best—fourth graders, Billy Rue.

In typical Brown fashion, however, I promptly did everything I could to squander whatever advantage there was in having two good players. (Both John and Billy would make the All-Star team.) You have to work hard to hide the talent of two players who are that good, but I managed.

Since a basketball court is small, you can't play all the kids at one time as you can in baseball. So the rules call for playing each kid at least half the game. Given that you have nine kids on the team, that doesn't give you much room to maneuver, as a little math reveals.

The games at this level are divided into eight three-and-a-half-minute periods, so by definition you only have forty slots to play your kids (the five boys who are on the court, times the eight periods).

But if each kid must play four periods—no matter how

good or bad they are—that means thirty-six of the slots are accounted for. (The nine kids, times the four periods they have to play.) That leaves you with just four "extra" periods. The question, of course, was: who would get that extra playing time?

For all the other coaches the decision was simple: you played your star, or stars, as much as you could. In some cases, the star would play all eight periods, and everyone else would play four. If you had two good kids, they'd each play six, with everyone else playing exactly half the game.

That decision made perfect sense. If you are playing basketball games where the final score is traditionally 22-18—throwing a regulation-size basketball into a 10-foot basket is not the easiest thing in the world to do if you are eight, nine, or ten years old—you want to get the ball into the hands of a kid who is good as much as you possibly can. That's why the stars played a lot more than anybody else on most teams.

On most teams, but not on mine. Nobody on our team played more than five periods, unless one of the kids was out sick.

For the most part, the parents of my kids thought my decision was cute. There was no reason not to. We lost our first three games, putting us three full games behind the league leader. With the season being only ten games long, it was clear to everybody that we had no chance at being league champions. Since that was the case, why not be magnanimous and play everyone equally? John Donovan's mother, Susan, and Billy Rue's dad, Bill—who was also my assistant coach—were the most supportive of all, even though my decision was costing their kids playing time.

So by game #4 all the pressure was off, and our kids—especially the low-rated ones—started playing a lot better. The result? We won four out of our last seven.

And that, as it turned out, was enough to get us into the playoffs.

Sort of. When the season ended, there were three of us with 4-6 records, so we were all tied for fourth place. (Only four teams made the playoffs.) That meant the three of us would have to play a round-robin tournament to determine who would get the fourth playoff spot, and with it the privilege of playing the number-one-rated team. (In our playoff system, as in the pros, the team with the best record plays the worst. The teams who finished second and third would play each other.)

The three coaches tied at 4-6 drew straws to see who would get a bye for the first round of our miniplayoff, and of course I didn't. Just to qualify for the playoffs, we'd have to win two games.

The first game of our minitournament was the next day, and the phone immediately started ringing off the hook.

"You are going to play Donovan all eight periods aren't you?" was the question everyone asked within ten seconds of saying hello. It was not an unreasonable assumption. John, in addition to being far and away the best third grader, was one of the best players in the league.

When I hesitated, I invariably heard this: "Fred (the coach of the opposing team) is going to play (his star) all eight."

People who just "happened to be driving by" the house stopped in to offer the same advice, and even my normally levelheaded wife started lobbying to play John more than the five periods he usually played. That would mean, I pointed out, that her son would only play four. "Fine," came the response. "Peter's only the fourth- or fifth-best kid on the team anyway." (That happened to be true.)

I knew I wasn't going to play John—whom I liked a lot—

all eight periods or even seven for that matter, but the discussion did give me a chance to explore something I had been wondering about ever since I started coaching: was there an easy way to predict who would take these games seriously and who wouldn't?

When I started thinking about it, I had assumed the breakdown would follow professional lines. Folks in competitive industries—investment banking, law, and the like—would treat the contests as, well, contests, placing great importance on who won and lost. Creative types, I figured, would be far less serious.

But that, I quickly discovered, wasn't true. And the more I explored the question, the more I found that other conventional classifications weren't predictive either. Whether or not you took the games seriously had nothing to do with your age, politics, or income.

It came down to gender.

One hundred percent of the guys I polled argued for playing *everyone* as much as you could, and every single woman— whether or not she had kids—recommended playing the star as much as possible, no matter what.

It may have been counterintuitive, but it *was* consistent.

The night before the game we had dinner with a friend of mine from law school, who had just made partner at a high-powered firm, and his wife, a woman I've known for fifteen years. I explained to Larry and Nancy the John Donovan conundrum and asked what I should do.

When Larry said, "You know, life is hard enough once your age has two digits in it, you don't need to make some of the kids feel inferior now," his wife all but broke his kneecap kicking him under the table.

As she listened to Larry, Nancy, who runs a huge bureau

175

for the state's largest newspaper, had a look on her face that said she had not been aware until this very moment that she had married a jerk.

"Life is tough and the kids should learn that right now," she said, as much to her husband as she did to me. "No one is going to coddle them when they get older. Besides, how are you going to feel if they don't win? Play Donovan."

And so it went down the line.

A Gucci-shod lobbyist, whom I went to college with, told me to play everyone equally. His wife, an accountant in a communications conglomerate, said, "Play the star all eight periods."

Women, for whatever reason, took these games much more seriously.

I sort of folded in the face of all this female "advice." I put John in for six periods and he promptly had a less-than-terrific game, primarily because there was too much pressure on him. Fortunately for us, Peter—who, as my wife correctly pointed out, is a much better baseball player—came through with two key baskets. More important, Keith McQuade, who turned himself into a great player (much to the detriment of his parents' ears) by spending hour upon hour dribbling a basketball in his basement, took charge. We won by one—in overtime.

We returned to our normal lineup the next game. One kid was out sick so everybody played five periods, and to the shock of everyone there—me included—we won our second straight. Billy Rue hit a layup with three seconds to go. (To this day, John Natale, the coach of the team we beat, mentions that shot every time I see him.)

Billy's basket got us into the finals and we promptly blew away the top-rated team.

It was the classic tortoise-and-hare situation. They were

176

the hares. They had ended the season 9-1 and were clearly the best team in the league. Nobody on their team—neither the kids nor the coach—took us seriously, and to be honest, I don't think I would have taken us all that seriously either.

So they came out overconfident and we came out in our plain-vanilla defense (a 2-3 zone for all you Bobby Knight fans out there) and we outscored them in every eighth. Keith McQuade ran the offense, taking all the pressure off John Donovan, who promptly responded with the game of his career. Everybody on our team scored at least one basket. And while the final score was 33-22, it was never even that close.

That got us into the finals, and while this one was a much better game, our team brand of basketball produced a 19-16 victory—in overtime.

What a shock! We were league champions. Peter, like everyone else on a winning team, ended up going home with a trophy that was just about as big as his sister.

I tell you all this to set up what happened as we gathered to start the next baseball season. There is a tacit understanding among all the coaches that whoever won the championship in the previous season (in this case, basketball) will not win it in the current one. He tends not to get the best players, his son's rating goes up a point or two and he is never given the benefit of the doubt on anything—all to assure he doesn't win again.

And I didn't.

At the third- and fourth-grade level the game changes substantially. For one thing, we have real umpires. (Okay, they're high school kids.) For another, the kids pitch.

One of the oldest clichés in the game is "baseball is 90 percent pitching." After this season, I'm willing to make that 99.44 percent. And we didn't have *any*.

When we were dealing out the cards on draft night, the long-

177

suffering Sherry Cavise, who again volunteered to be league president, insisted that every team end up with at least one kid who could pitch. (Invariably, the designated pitcher was a fourth grader who had pitched a little bit the year before.)

My pitcher was to be Adam Marinello, a bright, funny, talented ballplayer who only had one flaw. He had absolutely no intention of pitching. He had, indeed, done a little pitching as a third grader and he didn't like it.

Adam pictured himself as a first baseman—and in fact he made the All-Star team at that position. While I was thrilled that he could dream of being Will Clark, it left me with a serious problem. I had nobody who had ever pitched before. I gave everybody a shot at it and everybody was equally ineffectual. We had a team *earned* run average of 15.58, and that was being kind. More than half the runs that we classified as "unearned" quite easily could have been called the other way. To give you an idea of how bad it was: we *averaged* giving up nearly 2 hits *and* 2 walks *each inning*!

As long as I wasn't going to get any pitching, there was no reason for me to have any hitting either. While a team batting average of .297 sounds terrific, it was a good 100 points below the league average.

The statistics on the opposite page, compiled by David Sze, the world's best assistant coach, tell the entire story.

When you have no pitching and no hitting you're not going to win many games. And we didn't. We ended up going 2-9. There were not too many blowouts—we only lost three games by 6 runs or more—but still it made for a long season for the kids, and for me.

There were, however, a couple of funny moments.

One of the parents who had been giving all the first- and second-grade coaches a hard time—he basically thought we

Batting

Player	AB	Hits	Doubles	Triples	HR	Average
Peter	35	20	2	1	1	.571
Chris N.	28	13	2	0	0	.464
Adam	30	12	2	4	2	.400
Chris S.	31	11	4	1	0	.355
David	27	9	2	3	2	.333
Deepak	20	5	1	1	0	.250
Brian	29	6	1	0	0	.207
Jeff	27	5	1	1	0	.185
Mike D.	19	3	1	0	0	.158
Mike M.	27	2	0	1	1	.074
Nick	17	0	0	0	0	.000
Team	290	86	17	11	6	.297

Pitching

Player	Innings	Runs	Hits	Walks	Ks	ERA
Chris N.	16.3	20	26	25	29	11.04
Peter	11.7	15	21	9	15	11.52
Chris S.	2	3	3	5	4	13.50
Mike M.	16	26	25	26	23	14.63
Mike D.	1	2	0	5	2	18.00
David	4	9	11	6	5	20.25
Jeff	14	32	28	22	23	20.61
Brian	1	3	4	2	2	27.00
Deepak	1	6	5	3	0	54.00
Nick	0	0	0	0	0	00.00
Adam	0	0	0	0	0	00.00
Team	67	116	123	103	98	15.58

had no idea what we were doing—was named an assistant coach once his son became a third grader. And because fate can be cruel, he got assigned to one of the easiest-going coaches in the league. The assistant was gone by the third game, run off by the other parents who threatened to pull their kid off the team, if he didn't leave.

There was one game where a fourteen-year-old umpire ejected a coach, a guy who was a good foot taller than he was, for consistently arguing balls and strikes calls. On another occasion a mother who had been telling anyone who would listen—often at ten or eleven o'clock at night—how badly her son had been misused as a third grader, i.e. he never played shortstop and he always batted last—got a solid dose of reality. At the end of the season she was told politely, but firmly, that it would not be a good idea to let her son play on the fifth- and sixth-grade level. Given his lack of athletic ability, the kid was, in the words of one coach, "an accident waiting to happen." If he wanted to play, it was strongly suggested that he be held back and play with the third and fourth graders again. Sometimes justice does triumph.

On a more positive note, a suggestion I made seemed to be taking root. If a game is tied at the end of six innings, next year we are going to call it a tie instead of going into extra innings. "No reason for anyone to go home feeling bad" seems to be the consensus.

We've already rated the kids for next year and I'll be coaching again.

Maybe I'll see you at the ball park.